Presented To:

_____

_____

❦

From:

_____

_____

❦

Date:

_____

_____

❦

Through the Night
with God

Honor Books
Tulsa, Oklahoma

Through the Night with God
ISBN 1-56292-760-4
Copyright © 1999 by Honor Books
P.O. Box 55388
Tulsa, Oklahoma 74155

Contributing writers: Nancy Gibbs, Mary Ann Kerl, Patsy Ann Petree, Nanette
Thorsen-Snipes, and Rebecca P. Totilo.

Through the Night with God

with God

Night Glories

*Let my prayer be set forth before thee as incense; and
the lifting up of my hands as the evening sacrifice.*
Psalm 141:2 KJV

Some of the most fragrant flowers in the garden
stay tightly closed, or "sleep," during the day. They
open only later in the afternoon and evening,
perfuming the night air with their sweet scents.

The most magnificent of these late-bloomers is
the moonflower. Moonflowers look like white
morning glories, except that their blossoms are
enormous—up to eight inches across. Each bloom
lasts for only one night, but the scent more than
makes up for the short performance.[1]

Just as nature lends itself to day and night
creations, so there are "morning people" who feel their
best in the early hours of the day and "night people"
who seem to bloom after dark. If you are a late

bloomer, fill the night air with the sweet fragrance of prayer before God this evening.

The Lord looks forward to your companionship and is waiting to hear from you. Give Him your attention and listen to what He wants to tell you. Treat God as you would a dear friend.

Review your schedule to find time you can commit to God. Have no time? You may be overlooking some ready-made times, such as your drive to and from work or your coffee break. Find a place of isolation without distractions.

Jesus said, "Enter your closet" (Matthew 6:6 KJV). This "closet" can be any place, any time you can be alone with Him. Or you may want to designate one special place where you pray.

As you spend time seeking God during the night, you will bring a sweet fragrance into the throne room of God. The Bible describes this beautifully in Revelation 8:3: *And another angel came and stood at the altar, having a golden censer; and there was given unto him much incense, that he should offer it with the prayers of all saints upon the golden altar which was before the throne. (KJV.)*

Enjoy your night glories.

In Search of a Comet

*For as high as the heavens are above the earth,
so great is his love for those who fear him.*
Psalm 103:11

"Get up, kids," Andrea called. "Let's go see the comet!"

"What?" one of the twins asked. "Are you crazy, Mom? It's three o'clock in the morning."

"No, I'm not crazy," she said. "This is a once-in-a-lifetime opportunity. Get up. It'll be fun."

So the entire family fumbled into their clothes and went off in search of the famed Halley's comet. They finally parked in an open area that was free of city lights and filled with nature's night sounds.

As they stood leaning against the warm car, gazing up at the billions of stars sprinkled across the velvet black sky, sleepy eyes opened in wonder. The children pointed to first this light and then another. "Is that it?" they would ask. Yet despite a diligent search, no one could identify the comet. Apparently, its appearance was not as spectacular as scientists had predicted. Still the trip was worth it, and they excitedly continued to spot various constellations.

Andrea smiled and thought about how God's love is so much greater—so much more magnificent—than His creation. With her family together under the night sky, God seemed so close. She could feel the blanket of His love wrapped around her, keeping her safe.

On the way home, they stopped at an all-night donut shop and stuffed themselves with sugary treats. And later, the kids laughed and sang funny songs in the car. But only two hours after leaving home, they were tucked snugly back into bed.

Andrea thanked God for her family and the wonderful adventure they had shared as a result of a comet that they never saw. Some people would have called it a wild-goose chase, but she called it an opportunity to share God's wondrous creation with her children.

As she peeked into her children's rooms, what she saw was so much greater than Halley's comet. She saw the joy of love, the most glorious sight of all.

Worry Wednesday

Therefore do not worry about tomorrow, for tomorrow will worry about its own things. Sufficient for the day is its own trouble.

Matthew 6:34 NKJV

*M*any people lose sleep by worrying. They lie awake in bed, wondering if they made a right decision the day before—if they did the wrong thing—and what they should do tomorrow.

Here's a creative way one woman handled worry. With so many things to worry about, she decided to set aside one day each week to worry. As worrying situations occurred, she wrote them down and put them in her worry box. Then, on Worry Wednesday, she read through each worry. To her amazement, most of the things she was disturbed about had already been taken care of in some way. Thus, she learned there was seldom a justifiable reason to worry. As the psalmist wrote in Psalm 127:2, *It is vain for you to rise up early, to sit up late, to eat the bread of sorrows; for so He gives His beloved sleep* (NKJV).

American poet Ellen M. Huntington Gates described God's perfect rest for those with weary hearts in her poem "Sleep Sweet."

Sleep sweet within this quiet room,
O thou, whoe'er thou art,
And let no mournful yesterdays
Disturb thy peaceful heart.
Nor let tomorrow mar thy rest
With dreams of coming ill:
Thy Maker is thy changeless friend,
His love surrounds thee still.
Forget thyself and all the world,
Put out each garish light:
The stars are shining overhead
Sleep sweet! Good night! Good night![2]

As a child of God, you can rest in the knowledge that you are surrounded by a loving Father who cares for you. Jesus said, *Look at the birds of the air, for they neither sow nor reap nor gather into barns; yet your heavenly Father feeds them. Are you not of more value than they?* (Matthew 6:26 NKJV). Trust in God without fear or anxiety about what tomorrow may bring. The same Creator Who placed each star in the sky is watching over you.

An Angel in Deed

*Do not forget to entertain strangers, for by so doing
some people have entertained angels without knowing it.*
Hebrews 13:2

The hospital room was quiet. Natalie, who was
new to the area, was facing an emergency operation in
the morning. Knowing only a few people in this small
town added to her fear. She was alone in the hospital
room, unable to sleep, and as the night dragged along
she became more and more nervous. The quietness of
the room closed in on her.

She was ready to cry when she heard the creaking
of the door. She looked toward it and saw a kind
young face.

"Hi," the young woman said. "Are you lonely?"

"I sure am," Natalie replied.

"I'm a nursing student and have been observing
here for a couple of weeks. I've caught up on all my
paperwork. Do you feel like talking?" she asked.

"I sure do," Natalie replied gratefully. She straightened her pillow and slowly propped herself up in bed.

The compassion in the student's eyes comforted Natalie as their conversation soon turned to God and His wonderful and amazing grace. During the conversation, the heavy burden of fear in Natalie's heart began to lift. After a couple of hours, she finally drifted off to sleep. The young woman quietly left the room.

Natalie never saw the student nurse again. She couldn't even remember her name. But she never forgot the comfort and peace that settled over her as the young woman shared her love of Jesus Christ. The next morning, Natalie asked about the student nurse, but no one on the new shift had a clue as to her identity.

What had started out as one of the darkest nights of her life ended in peaceful contentment and sweet dreams, thanks to a young student with a kind heart. Whether the young woman was a celestial angel or an earthly angel of mercy, she was an angel in deed. She brought peace to Natalie's heart and joy to her soul. Isn't that precisely what God sends His angels to do?

Be a Blessing Counter

I will bless them and the places surrounding my hill. I will send down showers in season; there will be showers of blessing.
Ezekiel 34:26

"Oh no, not again," Wendy whispered to herself, as she awoke from a sound sleep at exactly two o'clock in the morning. For several nights now, she had awakened in the middle of the night unable to get back to sleep.

Wendy tried counting sheep forward and backwards, but she remained wide-awake. Warm milk only served to make her more alert. For several hours each night, she made herself miserable, trying to force herself to go back to sleep and worrying about the cause of her problem.

During the day, she found it hard to focus on her work, and the dark rings under her eyes made her look and feel much older than she was.

Then one night when she awoke during the early morning hours, Wendy picked up her Bible and began to read and study the Scriptures. For many nights to follow, she searched God's Word while gradually understanding the message it offered. Her sheep counting changed to blessing counting, and she discovered quickly that she always fell asleep before she could count them all.

Instead of dreading her insomnia, she now looked forward to studying God's Word in the middle of the night. His power and presence filled her soul. Gradually, the more time she spent with God, she gained spiritual power and increased her feeling of self-worth. For the first time in a long time, she felt in control of her feelings and began to believe that with Him she *could* do all things through Christ.

Eventually, Wendy's insomnia faded away, and her sleep grew sweet. She made sure, however, that she spent time alone with God during the day. But still she is grateful for the sleepless nights; God used that time to teach her the truth of living and the joy of loving. She learned, as she counted her blessings, that the answer to peaceful sleep is not in counting sheep but in calling on the Shepherd.

Born Free

For my yoke is easy, and my burden is light.
Matthew 11:30 KJV

James Forten, a fifteen-year-old slave, served
in the American Revolution as a powder boy aboard
the American privateer *Royal Louis,* a small ship
commanded by Stephen Decatur Sr. When offered his
freedom and a life of ease in England, the young sailor
from Philadelphia replied, "No, I'm a prisoner for my
country, and I'll never be a traitor to her."

The struggle for freedom did not leave any
lingering doubts in his mind. But some slaves must
have questioned it; after all, they were slaves—the
property of others. Why should they fight for liberty—
for independence and freedom? Freedom for whom? If
James had any doubts, though, they were drowned by

his belief that the Revolution was a path to freedom—
for all men.

Along with thousands of other slaves, Forten
endured tremendous hardship for many months during
the war. Finally, after being set free, he became an
inventor and manufacturer, giving much of his wealth
to aid poor and struggling blacks, and a founder of the
abolition movement, with the hope of ending slavery in
America. Forten's faith, courage, grit, and perseverance
helped bring a new, free nation into being.[3]

Many people today are still enslaved. The dark
chains of pornography, drugs, tobacco, and alcohol keep
them in bondage. For others, physical or emotional
abuse holds them in shackles.

But Jesus Christ can free you from the chains that
may be holding you in bondage. Jesus invites you,
Come unto me, all ye that labour and are heavy laden,
and I will give you rest. Take my yoke upon you, and learn
of me; for I am meek and lowly in heart: and ye shall find
rest unto your souls (Matthew 11:28-29 KJV). Find
freedom in Christ today.

Yesterday's Diapers

These things I command you, that ye love one another.
John 15:17 KJV

Patricia had a habit of ignoring others whenever she was particularly busy. One evening her husband complained, "I feel like yesterday's diapers." Patricia told him that she was simply busy and didn't mean to treat him badly, but as she fell asleep that night she thought about what he had said. Had she been ignoring him?

She thought about her busy days filled with changing diapers, grocery shopping, laundry, taking the twins to soccer practice, school plays, parent-teacher meetings, and volunteer work. She felt exhausted just thinking about it. Brushing off her husband's concerns, she dropped into a deep sleep.

Then one day she discovered for herself just how he felt. She had dropped by the offices of a well-known organization to leave some information. She had hoped to meet and talk with some of the volunteers, but to Patricia's surprise everyone was too busy to speak with her. Convinced that she was not welcome, she left in discouragement.

In our busy world, we often ignore one another. Many of us are overworked and overextended, and we find that it's easy to make a habit of ignoring others, including those we love the most. But we can make a difference in the lives of the people around us by taking the time to listen to them—by showing them that they are precious to God . . . and to us.

Jesus Christ said that the greatest commandment of all is to love one another, and that His followers would be known by their love . . . a deep and abiding love. So tomorrow, as you go about your day, take a moment from your busyness. Make a call and tell a friend that you think she's special. Not only will you brighten up your friend's day, you'll also speak volumes to a hurting and neglected world.

Never Diet Again

He that putteth his trust in the LORD shall be made fat.
Proverbs 28:25 KJV

It's you against all those fattening desserts: pies, cookies, cakes, candy. You have declared war on fat. You've carefully read food labels, measured portions, cut out the fatty foods from your diet and exercised regularly. But did you know there's an easier way to stay healthy and fit, one that doesn't require you to lose weight to accomplish your goals? In fact, God wants all His children to be FAT—spiritually speaking.

Here's how to gain spiritual weight:

F—Be *faithful* to do all that God tells you to do.

A—Be *available* for His use.

T—Be *teachable*.

God is calling you to be a faithful follower, one who will hold on to Him when life's problems are pressing in. You probably would rather run and hide. But what if God is transforming you into a stronger person through those trials? Would you still want to run? The stay-slim strategies of a physical diet require discipline, and the same is true in our spiritual walk with God.

Are you available for God's use? You may have given up time, money, family, and friends for Christ. Still, God wants you to give Him the things hidden deep within your heart—disappointments, hurts, and failings.

Are you hiding behind a wall of unforgiveness? Let go of past hurts and allow God to heal you. This will free you to help others. Replace old habits with good ones by seeking God's plan for your life.

Finally, be teachable. In 2 Timothy 2:15, we are reminded to: *Study to shew thyself approved unto God.* (KJV). Don't skimp on your daily nourishment from the Bible. Feed your spirit on God's Word every day and you won't feel spiritually hungry or deprived. When you end each day with a devotion and Scripture, somehow it dissolves all your problems and worries. So before you turn out the light, get FAT with God!

In the Dark

Then Jesus spoke to them again, saying,
"I am the light of the world. He who follows Me
shall not walk in darkness, but have the light of life."
John 8:12 NKJV

*D*id you ever go exploring through the woods as a child? Following an unfamiliar path seems like an adventure until it gets dark. While hiking up a mountainous trail, you lose track of time and murky shadows creep in. The sound of twigs and leaves cracking under your shoes grows deafening. Your great adventure now turns frightening. Suddenly, you can't see the path in front of you. If only another person would come along with a lantern and lead you back home.

Today, there are many people who walk in darkness. They are confused about their purpose in life and are searching for answers. They need someone to hold out a light and show them the way.

In the Dark

Psalm 18:28 says, *For You will light my lamp; the LORD my God will enlighten my darkness* (NKJV).

In our spiritual darkness of hopelessness and lack of direction, God promises to bring hope to our situation with His brilliant light of wisdom and understanding. Often that wisdom comes through the words of people we know or strangers we meet. Have you walked down a difficult road? Then share what God taught you in that situation. Lead others out of the darkness into a life filled with meaning and purpose. Share God's light with someone who is searching for the truth.

Do you work with young people? Share your experience and wisdom with them. Do you work in a hospital? Treat your patients as you would want to be treated in the same circumstances. Are you lonely and wish you had more friends? Volunteer. Share your God-given gifts and let your heart illuminate the lives of others. By helping other people find meaning for their lives, you'll discover God's purpose for your own.

It Is Well

When I lie down, I say, When shall I arise, and the night be gone?
and I am full of tossings to and fro unto the dawning of the day.
Job 7:4 KJV

During a time of unbelievable tragedy, Horatio Gates Spafford wrote a song of hope and faith. Spafford, a deeply spiritual man, built a successful law practice in Chicago just after the Civil War. He had five children: four girls and a boy. But like Job, Spafford endured great hardships.

Spafford's young son died of pneumonia. Four months later, Spafford lost all of his property and wealth in the Great Chicago Fire. After so much distress, Spafford's family planned a trip to join his good friend, Dwight L. Moody, in Great Britain. But unfinished business forced Spafford to stay behind while his wife and daughters went ahead by ship. On that voyage, Spafford lost all four daughters in a shipwreck, with only his wife surviving.

It Is Well

It was while sailing to join his wife that he received the inspiration for his greatest work and testimony. Looking out from the ship at the site where his daughters had drowned, he thought he couldn't bear any more pain. Then he recalled this Scripture: *For God so loved the world that He gave His only begotten Son* (John 3:16 KJV). Spafford realized that he would see his children again. Praying with a heart filled with that hope, Spafford uttered, "Whatever my lot, it is well with my soul."

Spafford put his thoughts on paper. After he and his wife returned home from Europe, Philip P. Bliss composed a tune to accompany Spafford's poem. The result is one of the best-loved hymns of all time.

If you think you cannot bear any more pain and feel all is lost, remember that God gave all He had and knows what you are facing. Read this beloved hymn and know that it is well with your soul:

When peace, like a river, attendeth my way,
When sorrows like sea billows roll
Whatever my lot, Thou hast taught me to say,
It is well, it is well with my soul.[4]

In the Garden

*For I reckon that the sufferings of this present
time are not worthy to be compared with
the glory which shall be revealed in us.*
Romans 8:18 KJV

The Garden of Gethsemane seemed darker that
night. During the day, visitors sat in the shade of its
olive trees beside slow trickling creeks to behold the
beauty of desert flowers. It was a place of rest—a
sanctuary for those who were weary.

But tonight its beauty brought Jesus no peace or
tranquility. On worn knees He knelt down, doubled
over in despair for that which He knew was soon to
come. Clenching His hands, His soul cried out to
God. The intensity of his agonizing prayer forced
droplets of blood through his skin to bead upon His
brow. Facing sure death by crucifixion, He asked of
His Heavenly Father, *Must it come to this?* But in the

hour of decision, He prayed, *Nevertheless, not my will but thine be done.*

It's comforting to know that when we dread tomorrow, our Lord knows exactly how we feel. He knows what it's like to be a father who takes a job he may dislike because it helps him put food on the table for his children. He knows what it's like to be falsely accused and wind up in court facing a judge and jury. He knows what it's like to be on the road and lose someone you love back home.

Because Jesus Christ endured this suffering for us, willingly accepting His fate, we have His assurance that He is always with us . . . He will never leave us or forsake us. For a hope in the heavenly life to come for us, He was willing to be the final sacrifice.

The end of His story is not found in the terrible beatings, the crown of thorns, the ridicule of an angry mob, or being nailed to the cross. The victory is that He died and was resurrected. His triumph is an empty tomb.

So tonight, whatever you're facing tomorrow, know that God is walking through it with you. Lean on Him.

God's Masterpiece

For now we see through a glass, darkly; but
then face to face: now I know in part; but
then shall I know even as also I am known.
1 Corinthians 13:12 KJV

French painter Claude Monet painted the world in a new way. In one of his most famous works, *Impression: Sunrise,* Monet used only color to create a composition. With no outlines, shapes were only suggested and blurred. His purpose was to catch a fleeting moment; moments later, the sun would be in another position, the small boat would have moved, and all would look different.

Working outdoors, Monet painted landscapes directly from nature. He had to work quickly, before the light changed, leaving little time to worry about fine detail. He wanted to catch just a glimpse of a particular moment in time. The altering light allowed him to see the same object in different ways. Monet often painted a series of paintings of the same subject to show these different appearances as the light changed.[5]

God's radiant light shapes our perspective of life. While we may not fully understand why we go through difficulties or changes in our life, the struggles we face on earth are fleeting moments compared to spending eternity with God. Difficult situations can sometimes blur our ability to see God's best for us, because we are seeing only a small glimpse of what God is doing.

Staring at the unfinished canvas of our life, we tend to miss the beauty of the masterpiece in progress. We may see only splashes of color without form or reason, never stepping back to visualize the entire spectrum of experiences that brought us to this point in our life.

Tomorrow, spend time in God's illuminating presence. It will refresh your outlook and give you a different way of looking at life's daily problems, as the Master completes the composition within you.

Pillars of Stone

Finally, beloved, whatever is true, whatever is honorable,
whatever is just, whatever is pure, whatever is pleasing,
whatever is commendable, if there is any excellence and if
there is anything worthy of praise, think about these things.
Philippians 4:8 NRSV

Hidden beneath the Chihuahuan Desert in New Mexico lies one of God's great wonders, Carlsbad Caverns. To the casual visitor its dark entrance can seem uninteresting, like the surrounding barren desert itself. Yet here is subtlety and grandeur, where over the centuries tiny drops of water, silently in the dark, built a startlingly beautiful monument forty feet high. Drop after drop, depositing particle after particle, a marble-like finger begins to grow. Ultimately, this process forms a tremendous pillar; thus, the cavern's sculptures are created.[6]

A similar process goes on inside each of us. As a single thought finds its way into our mind, it leaves

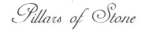
sediment that sinks deep down within our soul, forming our own pillars—pillars of character. If we let immoral, selfish, and violent thoughts fill our minds, we form eroding pillars of evil and failure. If we fill our minds with truth and love, we form strong and beautiful pillars within our souls.

In Proverbs 23:7, King Solomon said, *For as he thinketh in his heart, so is he* (KJV). Solomon understood that the things we dwell on determine the person we become. When we pursue God, we begin to reflect His character in our lives.

What formed the pillars of character in your life? Do you bear any resemblance to your Heavenly Father?

You can become the person God has designed you to be by renewing your mind daily in the Word of God. Just as the Carlsbad Caverns were developed over time, hidden from view, so our own true character is built.

Ruminating on God's Word

*This Book of the Law shall not depart from your mouth, but
you shall meditate in it day and night, that you may
observe to do according to all that is written in it.*
Joshua 1:8 NKJV

*H*ave you ever watched the news before going
to bed and then dreamed about one of the news
stories on the broadcast? The last thing we think about
just before we doze off settles deep within our
subconscious mind. Like clothes in a washing machine
on the spin cycle, thoughts spin around all night in
our minds. Then they often return to our conscious-
ness as the first thought we have in the morning.

King David said in Psalm 4:4, *Meditate within your
heart on your bed and be still.* (NKJV). Before you fall
asleep, think about God's Word and what God is doing
in your life. Ask yourself, what is the condition of my
spirit? Am I fulfilling God's plan for my life? That will

not only deepen your relationship with God, it also will expand your knowledge of Him.

Meditate—or ruminate—on God's Word as you lie on your bed at night. To ruminate, as defined by Webster's dictionary, means "to go over in the mind repeatedly and often casually or slowly." By spending time going over and over a Scripture, you can draw from it the depth of its meaning. The Bible reminds us to be transformed by the renewing of the mind.

So before retiring for the night, read a passage or two of Scripture. As you drift off to sleep, mediate on it. When you wake, you will have "ruminated" all night on God's Word, waking refreshed and renewed. Then in the morning, you can praise God as King David did: *My voice You shall hear in the morning, O* LORD; *In the morning I will direct it to You, and I will look up* (Psalm 5:3 NKJV).

The Lord Is My Shepherd

The LORD is my shepherd; I shall not want.
Psalm 23:1 KJV

A Shakespearean actor known for his recitations from the classics ended every performance with a dramatic reading of Psalm 23. Each night the crowd listened attentively. When he finished, the audience rose amid thunderous applause in appreciation of the actor's ability to bring the verses to life.

One night, just before the actor was to offer his customary recital of the psalm, a man in the audience spoke up. "Sir, do you mind if I recite the Twenty-third Psalm?" he asked. Confident that the man's talent was no match for his own, the actor allowed him to recite the psalm.

With a soft voice, the man read the psalm. When he finished, there was no applause, no standing ovation. All that could be heard was the sound of weeping. The audience had been moved to tears.

Amazed, the actor said, "I don't understand. I have been performing the Twenty-third Psalm for years. I have a lifetime of experience—but I have never moved an audience as you have tonight. What's your secret?"

The man humbly replied, "Well sir, you know the psalm . . . but I know the Shepherd."[7]

The Bible is not just good literature. It is truth. And it's not just enough to know the author of the Bible, Jesus Christ and His Holy Spirit. Knowing Christ means having a close relationship with Him. Following Jesus daily requires that you spend time with Him and study His Word to learn His ways.

Try to establish a routine of reading the Bible at the same time each day or night. Keep a journal of the passages you have read and how they apply to your life. Note all the special blessings God brings your way. And be sure to write down the way God answers your prayers. As you do this, you will begin to see the evidence of the Shepherd's leading in your life.

Ships in the Night

God hath given thee all them that sail with thee.
Acts 27:24 KJV

As Rebecca's one-year-old son, Dylan, played in the bathtub with his favorite toy—a little sailor—she silently asked God how they should spend the rest of the day. Every day seemed to be the same, a combination of errands and housework.

Dylan grabbed the sailor and plopped him in his boat, splashing water in Rebecca's face. Somehow, the splashing water reminded her that Navy ships had recently docked in their port city. "There are men in those ships!" she shouted.

Rebecca's family always enjoyed visiting the Navy vessels, but this time she sensed God directing them to minister to the six hundred servicemen who had been at sea for the last five months. But how? Rebecca

grabbed a towel and her dripping-wet baby and took off to go shopping for the newly arrived sailors.

As night drew near, her family climbed aboard a guided missile destroyer carrying gifts. The sailors, eager to see what was inside the green and gold boxes, greeted them. After the command duty officer was summoned on deck to receive their gifts, the officer offered to take Rebecca's family on a private tour.

To their surprise, when they visited the wardroom, they saw that one of the boxes had already been placed at the head of the captain's table. Trying not to notice, Rebecca quickly looked away, staring at a portrait. In the reflection of the glass, she watched an officer take something out of the box. She sensed the Lord whispering to her, *I want them all, so I start at the top.*

Lightly touching the rails, Rebecca's family prayed for each man who would hold that rail during the stormy seas of life. As the sailors lowered the American flag and illuminated the friendship lights, Rebecca's family bid them farewell.

Tonight, ask the Lord how He wants you to spend your tomorrow. Be available for Him. In doing so, you may touch many lives and make new friends.

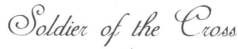

Soldier of the Cross

Fight the good fight of faith.
1 Timothy 6:12 KJV

Joseph, a seventeen-year-old patriot of the American Revolution, clutched his musket to his chest and leaned into the bitter wind. Exhausted, his eyes half-shut against the cold, he slipped on an icy rut. Valley Forge was twelve miles away; he realized the army had a long and painful march ahead of them.

This is how he described the circumstances: "We were literally starved. I did not put a morsel of victuals into my mouth for four days and as many nights, except a little black-birch bark which I gnawed off a stick of wood. I saw several of the men roast their old shoes and eat them. The army is now not only starved but naked. The greatest part were not only shirtless and barefoot, but destitute of all other clothing, especially blankets. . . . Hundreds of my companions had to go barefoot, till they could be tracked by their blood upon the rough frozen ground."[8]

The last few miles to Valley Forge were uphill, and the weary soldiers struggled to keep going. Because of the lack of supplies and the barrenness of the surrounding countryside, the men were without adequate shelter, food, or clothing; they lived in crude huts built by their own hands. Many died of starvation and cold. This was one of the darkest periods of the American Revolution. Yet it was at Valley Forge in February, 1778, that the army was trained, disciplined, and reorganized. And despite all the hardships they suffered, these soldiers continued the fight for America's independence.

How many of us today would endure such extreme hardships for our beliefs? During hard times, we are trained and disciplined to endure the stresses of life and appreciate the blessings of God. Tonight, ask God for the stamina to help and lead others to the kind of freedom that can only be found in Christ.

What Difference Can You Make?

I have planted, Apollos watered; but God gave the increase.
1 Corinthians 3:6 KJV

Annie, who worked with a homeless shelter, wondered if her efforts were making any difference to the men who spent most of their days living on the streets. How could carrying coffee or sandwiches to these destitute people make a lasting impact for Christ?

Yet she clung to the verse in which Jesus said, *For ye have the poor always with you* (Matthew 26:11 KJV). That was her excuse for not interacting with the homeless people as she served them. But still God gave her a special love for this group of people.

One day Annie ministered to a man named Vincent. He lived in a makeshift shack off a nearby boulevard. Everyone liked him—he was personable

and fun and a great talker. But like many people on the streets, Vincent had a drug addiction that controlled his life. His need for drugs drove him to break into downtown businesses to steal money; ultimately, he was arrested and jailed.

Volunteers at the homeless shelter visited him, and Vincent dedicated his life to God. A transformation took place in Vincent's life. Over the next couple of days, he single-handedly won more than eighty prisoners to Christ. When Annie heard the good news, her mind raced with possibilities for Vincent. But she never had time to work with him. On his third day in prison, Vincent died of a massive heart attack.

Although Annie didn't personally lead Vincent in his prayer of dedication to God, she was thrilled to share in the fruit of Vincent's harvest. Ministering and carrying sandwiches to Vincent proved to be time well spent.

Annie is just one person to whom God has given a special love for the homeless. Vincent was just one person with a heart of gratitude and a desire to share what God had done for him. Jesus was just one man, and through Him God saved the whole world.

A Child's Words

*Truly I tell you, whoever does not receive the
kingdom of God as a little child will never enter it.*
Mark 10:15 NRSV

Anne was visiting her mother one late winter
day when the temperature, which had given a hint of
spring that morning, took a drop back to freezing.
Anne had left home that morning with only a sweater
to keep her warm. Since she had other things to do
before going home, she asked to borrow one of her
mother's jackets.

Later in the afternoon, Anne went by the day-care
center to pick up her son, Jacob, a typical four-year-old
who usually gives his mother a full-blown account of
how his day went with the other children as soon she
picks him up. This time he noticed that she was wearing
the same kind of jacket that he was wearing, and he
asked where she got her new denim jacket. She told

him that she borrowed it from his grandmother. Jacob reached down and lifted the sleeve to his nose.

"Oh, Mom!" he said. "It smells!" She asked him what he meant. Did the jacket smell bad?

Jacob replied, "No, Mommy. It smells good—just like Grandma does!"

The next day Anne told her mother what Jacob had said, little realizing the impact her words had. To have a child identify you by smell evokes a personal and precious feeling; Jacob's comments made his grandmother feel loved in a special way.

Children accept us as we are, without any pretense. They expect us to be who we are and not the image we present to the world. That's the way God wants us to appear before Him. He already knows what we're going to say before we say it.

Tonight, be as direct as a child and tell Him precisely what you need and want. By speaking out your wants and needs, they will become obvious to you. God will hear you and respond in His time and in His way. He always answers your prayers.

The White Cane

*Rise in the presence of the aged, show respect for
the elderly and revere your God. I am the LORD.*
Leviticus 19:32

The first time Cathi saw Hank, a cantankerous old
man, he was leaning over the receptionist's desk with
his white cane raised high and yelling at the top of his
lungs. Part of Cathi's job as a caseworker for the state's
social services division was to visit elderly residents in
their homes, but Hank couldn't wait. He was letting
the whole office know about his problems.

Hank no doubt had been tall and robust before
age took its toll on his body. His eighty-year-old body
might have shrunk in stature, but his mind was still
sharp; and Cathi was just another thorn in his side
when she was assigned as his new caseworker.

Unsure of the reception she would receive, she
was filled with trepidation the first time she drove to

Hank's house. He acted out with his usual yelling and cane-waving, probably just to see how fast Cathi would run. Slowly she began to detect an undercurrent of sadness in the old man. Hank had outlived all his family and friends, including his wife. They had no children. Cathi thought of how lonely life must be for Hank. Maybe his cane-waving was a bid for attention, the way a two-year-old throws a temper tantrum for the same reason.

Over the course of the next year, Cathi visited Hank many times. She found him to be an intelligent man whose body had just gotten too old for him; he simply couldn't do the things he wanted to do.

We have much to learn from the elderly; they form a bridge from the past to the present and to the future. Do you have a "Hank" in your family or neighborhood? That person may suffer from loneliness, just as Hank did . . . and those feelings may intensify at night. Let "Hank" know that you'll be there, day or night.

The Empty Nest

Do not let your hearts be troubled. Trust in God; trust also in me.
John 14:1

Janet and Tom's younger daughter decided to marry right out of high school, although they would have preferred that she wait until she was older. However, Bobbie and her future husband felt they were ready to establish their own home together. Of course, there were the usual tears of joy and farewell as Janet watched them leave for their honeymoon.

What they hadn't counted on was the decision of their older daughter, Jackie, to move out of their home during the same week as her sister. That shouldn't have come as a surprise; after all, she was twenty-one and working. However, parents usually don't have to adjust to an empty nest all at once.

Janet walked past her daughters' rooms, now empty of their belongings, and was suddenly struck with the void in her life. Her daughters—her friends—were gone. She thought of the many experiences they had shared over the years, the times they laughed together, and the moves to faraway places as a family. She remembered a photo of Jackie in her Brownie uniform holding Bobbie, her little sister, by the hand. And she cried.

She knew that she and Tom would create new memories over the coming years. Bobbie and Jackie would return for visits, and they would talk endlessly on the phone. Yet Janet also knew it wouldn't be the same.

Some of the pain of separation was eased, knowing that they had done their best to give their daughters the knowledge and wisdom needed to make their own way in life. Both girls knew that their parents would always be there for them.

If you're facing a similar situation tonight, know that God is in control of the future. Some things will never be the same, but with the Lord in charge, your life can still be full and exciting . . . even if you now live in an empty nest.

Footprints

*Lift your drooping hands and strengthen your
weak knees, and make straight paths for your feet.*
Hebrews 12:12-13 NRSV

John loved to run and walk in the park
during the mild winter weather where he lived. So he
was surprised one morning in mid-January when he
discovered that the area had been covered with a
blanket of snow during the night. But since he was up
early anyway, John decided to go ahead and run on
the graveled jogging trail in the park. No one had
been out yet to leave footprints in the snow, but he
had been on the trail often enough to know its general
direction and its twists and turns. John forged a path
along the trail, leaving the prints of his shoes in the
snow. After several laps, other joggers joined him on
the course, following in his footprints.

Later that day, John returned to the park to walk his dogs. As he walked around the jogging trail, he noticed that the melting snow showed the route of the graveled trail in many places. It differed from the path of footprints. Now that the path was partially visible, people followed it rather than the footprints in the snow.

John thought about the way he lived his life. Most individuals follow an established way rather than forge their own path. It is a unique person who breaks away and makes his own footsteps. Did he know God's pathway well enough to walk it in uncertain circumstances? Did he set a course so that those who followed him would not be misled?

Tonight, ask yourself whether you know God's path for your life. All of us have doubts as we go through life, but if we study God's Word and keep our eyes on Jesus, we can follow in the footsteps of our faith. We can make footprints for those who come after us.[9]

Leave Them in God's Hands

Hear, O heavens, and give ear, O earth:
for the LORD hath spoken, I have nourished and
brought up children, and they have rebelled against Me.
Isaiah 1:2 KJV

Jeremy's mother heard the front door slam. Her son had ignored her directive to stay home and study for his math test in the morning. Sighing heavily, she wandered into his room, gazing at the gruesome music posters he had hung on his wall. Where was her happy little boy, who used to bring her bouquets of wildflowers in a grimy fist? Why had he become so belligerent and rebellious? Where had they gone wrong?

The room held no answers. She and her husband had attended church with him; Jeremy loved Sunday school. But when he turned sixteen, he dropped out of church and started hanging out with guys who dressed in black. Almost overnight, it seemed like her son had turned into a morose stranger. Weary, Jeremy's mother knelt by his bed and lifted up her heart to God in a three-word prayer, "Help me, Lord!" Prayer was her best defense against the darkness that was stealing her son. A peace settled over her heart.

When teenagers go astray and young adults go against everything that parents have taught them, the parents usually blame themselves. They ask, *Where did I go wrong? What could I have done better? What was the turning point? Should I have reacted differently to their rebellion? Was I too strict in my discipline?*

Even children with the most godly of parents sometimes rebel against God. We teach our children how to choose wisely, but the choices they make are theirs alone, right or wrong, and they bear the responsibility for them.

God has been in the parenting business for a long time. He understands about children going astray and choosing to make the wrong decisions. But God is the God of the second chance! Bring your children before the Lord often and allow Him to keep them in His hands. If they choose to wander off the path, He will know what to do.

What Really Matters?

Fathers, do not embitter your children,
or they will become discouraged.
Colossians 3:21

It was early in the morning on Father's Day, and four-year-old Joey and his six-year-old sister, Ginny, were fixing their father's breakfast. Ginny prepared Dad's favorite cereal, while Joey poured a glass of orange juice and placed it beside the cereal bowl on the tray.

Because they knew Dad liked to read the paper while eating his breakfast, his big sister sent Joey outside to bring in the paper and place it on the tray. Joey couldn't be expected to know that the most important section of the paper for Dad was the sports page.

Ginny carefully carried the tray into their parents' bedroom while Joey followed with a beautifully wrapped gift for Dad. Joey had only taken about three steps into the room, when he tripped and fell into

Ginny, spilling the orange juice all over the paper. When Dad saw his now unreadable paper dripping with juice, he yelled at both children, "How many times have I told you two to be careful and stop making a mess out of things?"

"Honey," his wife interjected gently. "Look at the breakfast they've made for you."

"I know—it's a mess!" Dad yelled. "Take it out of here!" The crying children left the room with their mother.

"He never even saw the present we had for him," Ginny cried.

"I know, baby." Their mother gathered the two children up in a big hug and kissed their tears. Ashamed of his behavior, their father stood over them and gathered his son up into his arms. "It's okay, Son."

From time to time, all parents are blinded to what really matters in the long term by the insignificant events of the moment. Orange juice on the paper, muddy tracks on the floor, and wet towels on the carpet are all frustrating. But there are times when God would rather we ignore the mess on the floor and see the gift in the child's hands.

Be Not Afraid

Commit your way to the LORD; trust in him, and he will act.
Psalm 37:5 NRSV

In the early 1960s, Jason was working in Oregon. One day in the winter, he took a group of young people from his church to hike in the mountains. Their parents were to pick them up at an old schoolhouse at two o'clock.

The sky was clear when they set out. But around noon, snow began to fall, and soon they could see no more than ten feet in front of them. Jason prayed for guidance and strength, then told the young people to hold on to one another. He urged them not to be afraid but to put one foot in front of the other and to keep praying. Slowly, they moved forward. After what seemed like hours, they finally made it down off the mountain and found themselves not far from the school.

Jason visited the Hood River valley again in 1992, where he met a woman from the church he had attended. She still remembered the expedition and told him that her memory of praying and putting one foot in front of the other had been an image that had guided her through many of life's stormy days.[10]

During our lifetime, we make millions of decisions. Some are small. Others are major, life-changing decisions regarding marriage, jobs, and education. We make most of these decisions based on the best information we have available at the time.

If you take your choices to the Lord and lay them before Him, He will help you to know what is in your heart and what your reasons are for making a decision. Some individuals are so afraid of making the wrong decision that they do nothing. Living your life to the fullest means communicating with God on a daily basis and continuing to put one foot in front of the other . . . regardless of the obstacles.

Renewed Vows

Remember that you and your wife are partners in
receiving God's blessings . . . You should be like one
big happy family, full of sympathy toward each other,
loving one another with tender hearts and humble minds.

1 Peter 3:7-8 TLB

The summer after high school graduation, Ellen and Michael were married in their home church. Everyone said it was a match made in heaven.

They both obtained jobs in their small town and soon were able to buy a house. After a few years, a little girl was born, and another year later, a baby boy. By this time, Michael had received several promotions, and Ellen was able to quit work and stay home with the children. Their family and friends all thought they had the perfect marriage.

As they planned their tenth wedding anniversary party, everything seemed to be going as scheduled—except Ellen and Michael didn't have much enthusiasm

for the coming celebration. They felt as if they were having the party for everyone but themselves. For the last few years, Ellen and Michael slowly had been drifting apart. Michael was involved with his job and Ellen with the responsibilities of the children and their home.

For the last four years, the couple had neglected to spend any time alone and seldom talked about any subject other than the children. However, the basis for their marriage—love and friendship—still existed. Michael and Ellen had simply let the process of daily living interfere with their feelings for each other.

On a lovely Sunday morning, their pastor gave a heart-wrenching sermon through which he seemed to be speaking directly to the couple. They were reminded of their love for each other and of God's love for His children. On the way home, they couldn't stop talking. They made the decision to renew their wedding vows in church and rededicate their lives to one another.

If your marriage is foundering in a sea of neglect, and you've failed to show your spouse the love you genuinely feel, make the decision tonight to renew your love and friendship, and let your life with each other flourish.

The Happiness Journey

Consider it all joy . . . when you encounter various trials,
knowing that the testing of your faith produces endurance.
And let endurance have its perfect result, so that you
may be perfect and complete, lacking in nothing.
James 1:2-4 NAS

We try to convince ourselves that life will be better after we finish school, land that great job, get married, or start a family. But then we're frustrated because the children are too young to allow us to do everything we want to, and we think that we'll be happier when they get older. Suddenly, we have teenagers to deal with, and we wish they would hurry up and get past that stage. We're sure that will make us happier.

We tell ourselves that our life will be better when we get a new car, buy a bigger house, and take that cruise we've always wanted to take. By then we've wished our youth away, and we tell ourselves that things will be perfect when we retire.

The Happiness Journey

The truth is, there's no better time to enjoy your life than right at this moment. God tells us that our lives will always be filled with challenges and trials. It's the way we react to these circumstances that makes the difference. Decide to be happy, no matter what.

Alfred D. Souza once said: "For a long time it had seemed to me that life was about to begin—real life. But there was always some obstacle in the way, something to be gotten through first, some unfinished business, time still to be served, a debt to be paid. Then life would begin. At last it dawned on me that these obstacles were my life."

Be happy with today while you plan for tomorrow. Happiness is the way, not the objective, so treasure every moment that you have. Spend your time with the ones you love.

Happiness is a journey, not a destination. God does not give us an infinite number of days—or nights—on this earth, so decide to spend each one in a way that pleases Him.[11]

Be Thankful

Praise the LORD! Praise the LORD from the heavens; praise
him in the heights! . . . Praise the LORD from the earth.
Psalm 148:1,7 NRSV

"Many times, I have read these suggestions:
Keep a record of the things that you are thankful for,"
Donald C. Everhart wrote. "Every morning, make a list of
God's gifts to you. At the end of each day, write on your
calendar one thing for which you can praise the Lord.

"For a long time, I hesitated. Counting my
blessings seemed too simplistic. On good days
thanking God seemed appropriate, but what could I
say to God on those awful days when I was depressed
or in trouble or when everything seemed to go wrong?
Surely I have many days when praise is not appropriate.
Finally, I tried it. Every day for a month, I wrote down
on my calendar one thing for which I was thankful.

Was I surprised! Even on routine, boring, and bad days, I could find a reason to praise God.

"I no longer keep a record on my calendar, but hardly a day goes by that I don't think of a good reason to be thankful. Keeping track of the things we are thankful for is one way to live in the spirit of the scripture."[12]

If you're lonely and discouraged with your life and looking for a reason to keep on living, hope is as close as the words of the Bible. Try the above suggestion for thirty days. Write down everything for which you're thankful—even if it's as simple as being thankful for the bluebird you saw in the park or the sight of a small child giving his mother a hug.

Sit on the porch at sunset or sunrise and see God's handiwork. As you look around at the earth and its beauty, you can't help but be aware of God's hand on your life.

In the words of Nathaniel Hawthorne: "Happiness is a butterfly, which, when pursued, is always just beyond your grasp, but which, if you will sit down quietly, may alight upon you."[13]

A Microwave Friend

*There are "friends" who pretend to be friends, but
there is a friend who sticks closer than a brother.*
Proverbs 18:24 TLB

When Sara was a little girl and went to visit her
grandpa, he would set her on the kitchen counter and
let her watch him make popcorn in the popcorn
machine. Those special times with Grandpa and the
popcorn machine were not to last. The problem was
not that Sara had grown too big to sit on the counter.
Rather, Grandpa discovered the convenience of
microwave popcorn. It was easy, cheap, and quick.

Now when Sara visits him, Grandpa asks her to put
a bag into the "micro" and "nuke" it. Sara eats the
popcorn, but she looks around the kitchen and there's no
Grandpa enjoying it with her. It only takes one person to
stick a bag of popcorn into the microwave. Sara misses
those precious moments of making popcorn with him.

A Microwave Friend

Have we become a generation of microwave friends? Friends who are here one minute and gone the next, like a fast-food hamburger. We used to call this type of friend an acquaintance—someone we met occasionally in our daily life—someone to have lunch with, meet at the same party, or see a movie with once in a while. It was enjoyable sharing our time with these people, but we knew they were not the friend who would sacrifice themselves to help us in a time of need.

The individual we could count on to assist us and whom we would sacrifice our needs to help in any and all circumstances was our true friend. This was the person we had spent time with, cried with, and rejoiced with—the person we had a history with and had taken the time to discover who and what he was like and what he believed in. A person who shared in the same belief system we did. Friendship is a relationship that stays strong no matter what.

God made us to need one another. Cultivate real friendships and weed out the phony ones.[14]

Bear in the Cave

My command is this: Love each other as I have
loved you. Greater love has no one than this,
that he lay down his life for his friends.
John 15:12-13

An old story tells the tale of two teenage boys who were cave exploring when they found what appeared to be huge bear tracks deep inside a long, cavernous tunnel. They decided to keep moving into the pitch-black cave, but crept ahead slowly and with extreme caution. Shining their flashlights into every dark crevice, they kept their eyes and ears open in case they actually encountered a bear.

Suddenly from behind a rock jumped the meanest looking grizzly bear they had ever seen. Standing up in front of them, the bear roared like a lion, sending a terrible sound echoing off the walls of the cave. The two scared boys scrambled back toward the front of the cave with the bear roaring behind them. Then one

of the boys dropped to the floor, quickly untied his hiking boots, whipped them off, and jammed on his running shoes.

His friend yelled at him, "Come on, man! Let's get out of here! Why in the world are you changing shoes? We don't have much of a chance of outrunning that bear anyway!"

Lunging to his feet and starting to run, the first boy replied, "I don't have to outrun the bear. All I have to do is outrun you."

Jesus said in the Bible that a friend is one who will give up his life for you, just as He did for all of us. But a fair-weather friend is one who will only be there for you as long as there's no risk involved. What kind of friend are you?[15]

Intentional Clutter

Then you will call upon me and come and pray to me,
and I will listen to you. You will seek me and find
me when you seek me with all your heart.
Jeremiah 29:12-13

As Angela cleaned her house one weekend, she wondered why on earth she kept so much stuff around that had to be picked up, dusted, or maintained in some other way. She spent hours during the week picking up papers, magazines, the television guide, and mail that hadn't been dealt with, along with the usual vacuuming, mopping, and laundering. She began thinking of ways to simplify her house to make her life easier at night and on weekends and free up more time to spend with her family. She vowed to stop letting clutter rule her life.

As she lay in bed thinking of ways to do this, Angela realized that her thought processes were as cluttered as the physical portion of her life. She recognized that she tended to rationalize, procrastinate, and fill up her mind with excuses to delay making important decisions. Her relationships with her husband and children were suffering because of all the emotional clutter filling up her heart. She never seemed to have enough time to spend with God. Angela had to admit to herself that clutter ruled her life. So she prayed and asked God to reorder her life.

Gradually, He helped her to clear away the years of clutter in her mind, emotions, and in her house. Instead of making excuses, she took time to read to her children and attend their school functions. Her husband benefited from a more loving and relaxed wife.

Think about ways you can clear up the clutter in your life. Use the extra time to create close, loving relationships with God and your family. Without all the clutter, it will be much easier to see the plan God has for you and to make your decisions in a way that is pleasing to Him.

The Tarnished Cup

Stop being mean, bad-tempered and angry. Quarreling, harsh
words, and dislike of others should have no place in your lives.
Instead, be kind to each other, tenderhearted, forgiving one
another, just as God has forgiven you because you belong to Christ.
Ephesians 4:31-32 TLB

After hours of searching through dusty cartons
in the basement, brushing aside spider webs and dust
bunnies, Kelly found the box that contained the baby
cup that had been her grandmother's. It was wrapped
in yellowed newspaper from many years earlier, as
evidenced by the dates on the paper. Kelly removed
the wrapping and discovered that the cup was now
blackened by tarnish. Frustrated and disappointed,
she stuffed the cup back into the carton.

That night Kelly was unable to sleep. After an hour
of tossing and turning, it finally occurred to her that she
was uneasy because her neglect and lack of concern had
allowed the cup to deteriorate. She got up quickly and

retrieved the cup from the basement. Finding some silver polish, she gently cleaned the cup until the beautiful silver again was revealed. With much work and love, she restored the cup to its original beauty.

Often our relationships with family and friends tarnish and deteriorate under layers of hurt feelings, anger, and misunderstanding. Sometimes the deterioration begins with a comment made in the heat of the moment, or it may begin under the strain of other stresses. If the air isn't cleared immediately, the relationship tarnishes.

When we put work and love into our relationships, they can be restored. Then we rediscover the beauty that lies underneath the tarnish and realize that it has been there all along.

If you're lying awake tonight, unable to sleep because you've been hurt by a loved one or you've said hurtful words or retaliated in kind, remember the teachings of Jesus and ask forgiveness for yourself and your loved one.[16]

Love's Variety

And now these three remain: faith, hope
and love. But the greatest of these is love.
1 Corinthians 13:13

Late Saturday afternoon, with shadows lengthening in the garden, Linda stretched her back and wiped the sweat from her brow, gazing at the newly turned soil in the rose bed. She had spent the entire afternoon pruning, planting, or fertilizing every pansy, hollyhock, and evergreen in the yard, but it was growing dark and it was time to quit.

After making a glass of iced tea, she lay back in the chaise on the deck to watch the fireflies flicker in the tall ornamental grasses. How she loved the infinite variety of God's creation!

There was something about digging in the soil that turned her thoughts to the Creator, maybe because God was the first Gardener—the Vine Dresser. And he

Love's Variety

had planted such a variety of love in the world: the love of a spouse for a mate, the love between parent and child, the love of a friend for another. Linda remembered her father, a quiet man, who had been killed in Vietnam. Out of love for his country, he had died a hero.

However, she knew that the most unselfish love of all is the love Jesus has for each individual. She was so grateful that His love was the cornerstone of her life and the foundation of her existence—the Rock on which she anchored her love for others. Every experience she faced and every new person she met, she tried to see through His eyes, and when she did, she found it added a whole new dimension to the way she was able to love people. Even when she feared or disliked someone, God's love allowed her to find new opportunities to share His love with those people.

In your quiet time with God tonight, ask Him for the gift of love and share it with someone else tomorrow. Become a person of faith and hope, but most of all, become a person of love.[17]

A Solid Ice Sheet

He alone is my rock and my salvation; he is my fortress,
I will not be shaken. My salvation and my honor
depend on God; he is my mighty rock, my refuge.

Psalm 62:6-7

An Environmental News Network report released in late 1998 indicated that contrary to what some people believe, the Antarctic ice sheet is not melting rapidly and has been stable for more than a century. The ice sheet is the largest grounded repository of ice on the planet, and some scientists have argued that the melting of this ice sheet would lead to a dramatic rise in sea levels.

Many feared that a global warming would melt this ice sheet, causing widespread flooding. Politicians, working with naturalist groups, passed legislation to limit growth and production. Predictions were made that cities located near the oceans would be flooded and farmlands ruined.

The news report may ease fears for a while—until some new report comes out. But it seems that the huge ice sheet will be around for a lot longer. It's massive and solid.

God, on the other hand, has been around for far more than a century, and He will never break away from humanity. God will calm our fears and ease our trepidation. As our Rock, He will give us the wherewithal to deal with all of our circumstances, no matter how tough they may seem. God is not a cold, icy experience, and He will not wear away like the drip of water on stone.

Your life may be unsettled and stormy, causing you to feel as if you were bouncing about on rough waters. But if you allow God to enter your life, He will melt away your fears and concerns and bring a spring-like freshness to your heart.

As you meditate tonight in preparation for sleep, let God help you prepare for tomorrow. Pray to Him for guidance in your daily decisions. Let Him be your guiding hand in all you do. Let Him rock you gently to sleep, and trust Him to bring you through the rough waters tomorrow. Let Him be your rock and your refuge.[18]

Grandpa Understands Me

*Let your light shine before men, that they may see
your good deeds and praise your Father in heaven.*
Matthew 5:16

Jim and Elaine considered themselves blessed
to be able to spend a weekend with their daughter and
her family, whom they didn't see as often as they
would like. After a drive of several hundred miles,
they checked out the house Sandy's family would be
moving into the following month, played a round of
miniature golf, and enjoyed a lovely dinner together
that evening.

Before they left the next morning, their grandson,
eleven-year-old Nicholas, asked Jim to play a computer
game with him. Nicholas had always been close to both
of his grandparents, but he and his grandpa usually
spent a lot of time together whenever Jim and Elaine
visited. After they finished their game, Elaine made a
comment about how long it had taken to play.

"Grandpa and I spent a lot of time talking," Nicholas said, leaning against his grandmother's chair.

"About what?" Elaine asked.

"Nothing much," Nicholas replied. "Grandpa just understands me and how I feel about things."

Elaine gave a lot of thought to her grandson's words, thanking God that Nicholas had such a close relationship with his grandfather—someone who accepts him for who he is and sets an example for him.

Too often our lives are so busy that we don't realize the effect our words have on others, especially on our family. We see them every day, and they mirror our attitudes, whether good or bad, negative or positive. How many times have you heard a small child repeat something inappropriate that an adult has said in front of him?

What does your mirror reveal to your children or your grandchildren? Does it set a high standard for them to follow? Ask God tonight for His help in establishing that high standard.

The Butterfly Inside

Dear friends, let us love one another, for love comes from God.
Everyone who loves has been born of God and knows God.
1 John 4:7

*J*ean Thompson stood in front of her fifth-grade class on the first day of school and told them that she loved each child in the class equally. But she knew that wasn't entirely true, because there in front of her was a little boy named Teddy Stoddard.

Mrs. Thompson had watched Teddy the year before and noticed he didn't play well with the other children. His clothes were unkempt, and he always seemed to need a bath.

When Mrs. Thompson reviewed Teddy's records, she found that his first-grade teacher had written, "Teddy is a bright, inquisitive child." His second-grade teacher wrote, "Teddy is well-liked by his classmates, but troubled because his mother has a terminal illness." His third-grade teacher wrote, "Teddy continues to work hard, but his mother's death has affected him." Teddy's fourth-grade teacher wrote, "Teddy is withdrawn. . . . "

At Christmas, Teddy brought Mrs. Thompson a present. She opened the package and found a rhinestone bracelet with some of the stones missing and a partial bottle of cologne. She mentioned how pretty the bracelet was and dabbed some of the perfume behind her wrist. Teddy said, "Mrs. Thompson, today you smell just like my mom used to."

Just as Mrs. Thompson realized that she had let Teddy's physical appearance and poor attitude color her judgment of him, many of us are guilty of doing the same thing at times. The words and actions of other people can wound a tender spirit, especially that of a child.

As you reflect upon your day, how did your actions impact other people? It's important to remember that Jesus loved everyone regardless of position in life, character, intelligence, or physical beauty. The Bible says, "Love thy neighbor." It doesn't say love them only if they're pretty, or the mayor, or the minister. Remember, there is nothing in a caterpillar that tells you it's going to be a butterfly.[19]

The Night Shift

Behold, bless ye the LORD, all ye servants of the LORD,
which by night stand in the house of the LORD.
Psalm 134:1 KJV

Ah, the moon is up. Doesn't that make you feel like getting up, eating breakfast, and going off to work?

No? Then you're like most people who naturally want to sleep at night, and work and play during the daylight hours. But for some, their jobs require them to march to a different beat—to sleep during the day and be alert, active, and productive at night. While the world sleeps around them, many are up working the night shift.

If you are among those who must work late at night, life may seem lonely. Your clock is set for an evening wake-up call, while others are set for the morning. If a friend suggests playing tennis at noon, you know you'd feel more like it in the middle of the night, but you'd have a tough time finding a willing friend and a court lit up in the wee hours of the morning.

At times, it may seem like a friend is nowhere to be found. You are not alone though. God is a friend who is always there for you. No matter whether it is day or night, you can spend time with God because He never slumbers nor sleeps.

During the dark nighttime experiences of life, it may not be easy to praise God. But it's during these dark seasons that God puts a song in your heart. Psalm 77:6 reads: *I call to remembrance my song in the night* (KJV). God replaces your discouragement with a song.

While imprisoned in Philippi, Paul and Silas were able to lift up their hands and voices in praise to God after being beaten and placed in stocks. They were on the night shift, and God heard their prayers and praise and sent deliverance. You, too, are serving God on the night shift. He will hear and answer your prayers as well.

A Heart at Home

*If anyone loves me, he will obey my teaching. My Father will love
him, and we will come to him and make our home with him.*
John 14:23

Throughout his life, Glen worked hard. In
addition to his regular full-time job, he worked as an
automobile mechanic. It didn't matter what hour of
the day or night his customers needed his help, he
was always ready to come to their rescue. Diligently,
he worked to get their cars running again.

He looked forward with eagerness to his
retirement. He wanted to travel around the country
and show his wife all the things that she had only
dreamed of seeing. While he used the money that he
earned at his full-time job for bills and living
expenses, he saved every dime he made repairing cars.
He called that his honeymoon account. He had never
taken his wife on a formal honeymoon, and he

intended to begin their trip right after he retired. He was so proud of himself for planning their vacation of a lifetime.

When Glen realized how much he had saved, he was amazed. He had enough money to buy a recreational vehicle, with money to spare. After he made the purchase, he and his wife left for their long-awaited honeymoon. They were gone for only a few days when, to everyone's surprise, they returned home.

"There's just no bed like ours," Glen said when others asked why he was back so soon. "When the sun went down, we both missed home so much." With a twinkle in his eye he said, "Home is where the heart is, and my heart is here, especially at night."

Before long, Glen could be seen in the wee hours of the morning laboring over yet another car. With a renewed smile on his face, he sold the recreational vehicle and made a promise to his wife. "Until God calls us to our home in the sky, we'll never leave this place again, honey. There's simply no place like home."

Fiery Trials

And the fire will test each one's work, of what sort it is.
If anyone's work which he has built on it endures, he will
receive a reward. If anyone's work is burned, he will suffer
loss; but he himself will be saved, yet so as through fire.
1 Corinthians 3:13-15 NKJV

On the slopes of the rugged Sierra Nevada, the giant sequoias inhabit a forest realm that they have ruled for millennia. From the mists of the ancient past they have emerged—the largest of all living things on earth—a symbol of an incredible will to survive.

Over the thousands of years the sequoia have existed, they have had to make changes in order to endure. The most important of these adaptations have to do with fire, since lightning storms are common in the foothills of the forest.

These trees have developed a thick, fire-resistant bark, which burns poorly and protects them from the intense heat generated by fires. Although a particularly

hot fire may succeed in burning a tree and leaving a scar, a healing process begins almost immediately. New bark creeps over the wounds until the breach is covered and fully protected again.

Natural fires also provide optimum conditions for germination. Hot updrafts dry and open old cones, releasing seeds that shower the forest floor. The freshly burned floor, now cleared of undergrowth and competing trees, allows the seedlings access to sunlight and minerals in the soil.[20]

The fires, or trials of life, that we endure also help to burn away the undergrowth and weeds of our faults that prevent us from growing and maturing in the Lord. Weeds such as greed, pride, and ungratefulness must be removed in order for us to bear fruit in our lives.

Just as the seedlings need sunlight and minerals to survive, we thrive on God's light by entering His presence through prayer and receive nourishment by reading His Word daily. Although the trials of life are painful to bear, God is there to begin the healing process and fully protect us during those times.

Savor the Moment

So teach us to number our days, that
we may apply our hearts unto wisdom.
Psalm 90:12 KJV

$\mathscr{A}$nn described a lesson she learned after the painful loss of her sister. Her brother-in-law opened the bottom drawer of her sister's bureau and lifted out a tissue-wrapped package. "This," he said, "is not a slip. This is lingerie." He discarded the tissue and handed the slip to Ann. It was exquisite silk, handmade and trimmed with a cobweb of lace. The price tag, bearing an astronomical figure, was still attached.

"Jan bought this the first time we went to New York nine years ago. She never wore it. She was saving it for a special occasion. Well, I guess this is the occasion." He took the slip from Ann and put it on the bed with the other clothes they planned to take to the funeral home. His hands lingered on the soft material for a moment, then he slammed the drawer shut and turned to Ann. "Don't ever save anything for a special occasion. Every day you're alive is a special occasion."

She remembered those words throughout the funeral and the days that followed. Ann thought about all the things that her sister had done without realizing they were special. The words her brother-in-law spoke changed her life.

Ann now spends more time with her family and friends and less time in committee meetings. Now she enjoys the view from her deck without fussing about the weeds in the garden. She's not saving anything either; her family uses the good china and crystal for every special event . . . such as losing a pound, unclogging the sink, or spying the first camellia blossom of the season.

As you watch the breathless beauty of a sunset or the colorful splendor of a rainbow, savor the moment. Cherish the brilliance of the maple leaf nipped by frost and the white clouds floating across the crystal blue sky. Remember that every moment of every day is special.

Grandmom's Angels

For he will command his angels concerning
you to guard you in all your ways.
Psalm 91:11

Kathleen Lowthert described a special conversation she had with her granddaughter at a critical time in Kathleen's life.

Kathleen, who was scheduled to have an operation several days later, was joined by two-year-old Shanice one day as she was having her daily devotions. After reading her Bible and praying, Kathleen began reading some information about the anesthesia she would receive prior to surgery. The more she read, the more she realized how nervous she was about the operation.

That's when Shanice looked at her and said, "Grandmom, show me the angels."

"Angels?" Kathleen asked.

Then Shanice pointed to a photo on the cover of the brochure Kathleen had been reading. "No, Honey," Kathleen said. "That's a doctor, a nurse, and a patient."

"Yes, Grandmom—angels," Shanice replied.

Her granddaughter's simple misunderstanding proved to be a powerful reminder to Kathleen that God would, indeed, give His angels charge over her. She decided right then that she would not waste another moment worrying about the operation but that she would praise God instead. A supernatural peace flooded over her as she thanked God for the protection she knew He would provide during her stay in the hospital.[21]

Kathleen vividly saw how children can remind us of the simplest truths. There are times in all of our lives when we worry about our families, health, finances, job, and the many decisions that we may have to make on a regular basis. We spend more time worrying about the problem than taking steps to solve it. Are you unable to sleep because you can't stop thinking about your problems? It's time to take that next big step.

Put yourself in God's hands tonight and pray that He will lead you to the right action. Then simply let go and trust Him, believing that you will sense God's direction and that He will bring you the peace you need.

A Few More Hours

Simon answered, "Master, we've worked hard all night and
haven't caught anything. But because you say so, I will
let down the nets." When they had done so, they caught
such a large number of fish that their nets began to break.

Luke 5:5-6

David and Lynn were getting discouraged. The restaurant they owned was foundering even though they had extended their business hours and offered special dinners, hoping to attract more customers. But no one came.

After several weeks with no change in sight, Lynn said, "We might as well close up and go on home." It was nearly eleven o'clock.

"Let's stay open a few more hours," David suggested.

"Why?" Lynn frowned. "What's the use?"

"Because tonight may be the night we get more customers." David grinned, and his wife noticed the hope shining in his large hazel eyes.

A Few More Hours

Even though Lynn didn't relish the idea, she agreed that they should keep the restaurant open.

About thirty minutes later, a miracle seemed to occur. A late evening bus drove into the small community and stopped in front of the café. People poured out of the bus and into the cold winter air. Quickly they entered the warm café, since it was the only restaurant still open.

The profits David and Lynn made that evening helped compensate for some of their earlier losses. But that was only the beginning.

Soon word spread that the small restaurant stayed open late at night. Business came from all around—people driving through the town late at night, buses passing through, late-night railroad crews. The couple even had to hire an extra waitress for the late shift.

Sometimes when we've worked late in the night and are ready to give up, if we wait patiently, we will reach our goals. What we long for may arrive within minutes. Take comfort in the fact that we don't know what tomorrow brings. It could be a special day—or night—for us.

Anybody Home?

The LORD's curse is on the house of the wicked,
but he blesses the home of the righteous.
Proverbs 3:33

Jennifer was resting after returning home from a weekend retreat with her husband when she heard the door open.

"Hello!" a familiar voice said. "Anybody home?"

Both Jennifer and Kevin hurried to the door to greet their daughter. At twenty years of age, Becky was trying to discover her place in the world. Gradually, she was attempting to let go of her parents and enter a world of new beginnings.

Letting go of their children had been difficult for the couple. Since Becky was the baby of the family and the only girl, it was even more difficult. Jennifer had spent many sleepless nights worrying about her daughter. At night when Jennifer would hear the door unlock, signaling Becky's safe return, she would whisper a prayer of thanks to God for placing His protective hand over her.

As the nights passed, she learned to depend on God more and more. She realized that even though she couldn't be with Becky every moment of every day, God could. Over the previous year, she had placed her daughter into the hands of God, allowing Him to guide her steps. This made the nights a lot less worry-filled.

"I'm glad you're home," Becky said as she hugged and kissed her mom and dad. "I missed you both so much." They had only been away for two nights, but to Becky it seemed like an eternity. While she wasn't home much herself, she wanted her parents to be nearby just in case she needed them.

Aren't we glad that God is always home? He never leaves our side and always offers the security that we need to live each day to its fullest. Through the darkness of the night and the brilliance of the day, He remains faithful and true. Thank you, God, for living with us in our home, the greatest earthly gift ever given.

Consider the Heavens

*When I consider your heavens, the work of
your fingers, the moon and the stars, which you
have set in place, what is man that you are mindful
of him, the son of man that you care for him?*
Psalm 8:3

Astronomers keep finding light in our dark universe.

Helen Sawyer was born in 1905 in Lowell, Massachusetts, and twenty-five years later married Canadian astronomer Frank S. Hogg. Noted for her research on what are called variable stars, Helen found more than two hundred and fifty such stars that display different degrees of brightness.

Receiving her doctorate in astronomy from Radcliffe College in 1931, Helen studied globular star clusters in the Milky Way galaxy. By studying the variable stars, she was able to determine the time required for some of these stars to change from bright light to dim light and back to bright light again. This information helped other scientists to calculate the distance of certain stars from the earth.

For centuries, scientists have discovered more and more information about the light at night in our huge universe. Today scientists know that the heavens contain a mind-boggling number of stars, moons, planets, and galaxies. Most are far beyond what the naked eye can see, and much of the light in our night sky can't even be seen with today's powerful and gigantic telescopes.

Think of all the night lights discovered during your lifetime. Then think of the night lights still waiting to be discovered. There's no way to predict how much more future astronomers will find out about our vast universe.

Tonight, try to count the number of stars you can see out of your window. Study the moon with a telescope, or search for the Big Dipper, the Little Dipper, the North Star, and other famous constellations. As you enjoy light at night, you'll inevitably come to appreciate the tremendous amount of light God has provided in the universe.

Are You Rich?

*The sleep of a laborer is sweet, whether he eats little or much,
but the abundance of a rich man permits him no sleep.*
Ecclesiastes 5:12

Amy, a young mother, longed to be rich, thinking that wealth would ease the financial strain on her self-employed husband. They lived in a moderate middle-class home, but Amy wanted a more expensive one.

One day Amy visited her sister in her new home, and she was impressed. A chandelier hung from the dining room ceiling. The kitchen featured every built-in appliance and gadget possible. The den boasted a large-screen television, loads of CDs, and an enviable stereo system.

Amy thought, *Joe and I could enjoy a home like this, too, if I went to work.*

Later, after the tour of the house was over, Amy asked her sister what time she had to get up for work every morning.

"Five-thirty," Janice said.

Back in her own home, Amy looked at her husband with tears of gratitude in her large brown eyes.

"Do you realize how rich we are?" she asked Joe.

"What do you mean?" Joe frowned.

"I don't have to get up early in the morning and leave our precious son at a sitter's house. I can enjoy him all day. I'm rich! I just never realized it before."

Joe laughed, grabbed Amy, hugged her and said, "I totally agree."

In our society, it's so easy to get caught up in material things. Everywhere we look, advertisements appear before us, enticing us to buy a beautiful home, luxurious furniture, designer clothes, late-model cars, boats, motorcycles, and cosmetics.

Tonight, take a look at your surroundings. Notice how rich you are . . . maybe not with expensive, material objects, but with the things that count. Do you have a pile of library books on your sofa? Or nutritious foods in the cupboard? Or maybe on your refrigerator you have a priceless photo of your child.

No matter what you own, take note of your blessings tonight and enjoy them.

Visible Blessings

*So then, just as you received Christ Jesus as Lord, continue
to live in him, rooted and built up in him, strengthened in the
faith as you were taught, and overflowing with thankfulness.*
Colossians 2:6-7

Marilyn and Velma were two young mothers
who lived across the street from each other. From their
living room windows, each woman was able to observe
the activities of the other woman's family.

One day, Marilyn confessed that she'd been
watching what went on in Velma's front yard and that
she envied her.

"I don't know what you mean," Velma said with a
puzzled look on her face.

"Well, I often see your husband out in the front yard
mowing your lawn, and I wish my husband would do
the same thing," Marilyn said. "Your yard is beautiful."

Velma laughed and then made *her* confession.

"I've been doing the same thing," she said. "I watch your husband in your front yard—and I've envied you!"

Marilyn shook her head. "What on earth do you mean?"

"I see your husband playing ball with your toddler so much. How I wish Keith would do the same thing! He never wants our boys in the way when he mows. Be honest, Marilyn. Wouldn't you rather have your husband playing with your son than a well-manicured lawn?"

"I hadn't thought of that before, but you're right. I may have tall grass, but Eric is good about playing with Johnny," Marilyn said.

Sometimes we are blind to blessings that are so obvious to others. Tonight, we can take an inventory of our blessings and be thankful for those we have in our lives. Perhaps there's a blessing or two—or even more—you hadn't thought about until just now. Talk to God about that tonight, thanking Him for all your blessings, both seen and unseen, that He has given you.

Inner Strength

For you remember, brethren, our labor and toil; for
laboring night and day, that we might not be a burden
to any of you, we preached to you the gospel of God.
I Thessalonians 2:9-10 NKJV

When Bill's unit was dispatched to Vietnam, the
first problem he encountered was his inability to get
enough sleep. He worked most of the day and night in
a hot and humid jungle environment that left him
drained of energy. Sometimes late at night he would
fall asleep while writing a letter to his wife, whom he
had married not long before he left home to fight in
the war. This pattern went on for weeks.

Bill watched other men work hard, too, even
though they also got little sleep. Day after day and night
after night, the men courageously fought in the muggy
jungle, dodging tree branches as they ran carrying
heavy equipment. Without complaining, Bill continued
to work in the damp jungle. Sweat poured through his
fatigues as he went from one assignment to the other.

Like the other men, Bill didn't have the opportunity to bathe as often as he would have liked, and mealtime was usually quick and straight out of a can.

After several months spent in the jungles of Vietnam, Bill noticed that he was capable of doing so much more than he ever dreamed possible—physically, emotionally, and spiritually. He learned that he had an inner strength and power he'd never depended on or called on before.

Soon Bill was able to make wise decisions regardless of the amount of sleep he had gotten, because he started believing and telling himself that he could do whatever needed to be done, no matter how tired he was. Finally his tour in Vietnam was over, and he had survived.

God said in the Bible that if we keep our faith in Him, then all things are possible. All of us are capable of drawing on great energy reserves and developing faith in ourselves just like Bill. Whatever obstacles we face—especially at night—we can find courage within ourselves to confront those difficulties in our lives . . . with God's help.

Keeping Watch

But understand this: If the owner of the house had known at
what time of night the thief was coming, he would have kept
watch and would not have let his house be broken into.

Matthew 24:43

"*W*hy aren't you asleep?" a prison inmate yelled
at a guard who was being held hostage during a riot at
a maximum-security prison. "It's the middle of the night!"

At age sixty-three, the guard, Alex, was the oldest
hostage. Even though he had fought in three wars and
had been trained for combat, he was scared.

"I'm not sleeping because I've been taught that
sometimes it's necessary not to sleep at night but to
stay awake," Alex told the inmate. "I figured tonight
was such a situation. I'm looking out for my safety. I
want to be able to defend myself if an inmate bursts in
here and tries to kill me."

Then a strange thing happened. The inmate
studied Alex for a moment and said, "You're a smart

man." Instead of attacking Alex with the homemade knife he held, the inmate left the guard in the cell.

Alex watched other inmates run back and forth. His heart pounded. He didn't know from one moment to the next what was going to happen. He thought of his family and friends. He had no idea if he'd see them again. Unlike some of the other hostages, Alex escaped the situation without injuries even though about sixty inmates were armed with homemade knives during the two-day riot.

Sometimes we have to be awake at night even if we'd prefer to be sleeping. Maybe you're one of those people. Your situation probably isn't as dramatic as that of the prison guard.

But whatever the reason you are up tonight, find satisfaction and peace in the knowledge that eventually you will be able to sleep and get the rest your body requires. Sometimes it's necessary not to sleep at night but to stay awake, being ever vigilant in the task God has set before you.

Little Things

Then they cried to the LORD in their trouble, and he
saved them from their distress. He sent forth his word
and healed them; he rescued them from the grave.
Psalm 107:19-20

One day as Sarah tugged and pulled to rearrange
the furniture, she injured her back, ending up with
two slipped discs. She went to the doctor, who told
her to alternate placing an ice pack and moist heat on
her lower back. Even though Sarah followed his
directive when she got home, she woke up in middle
of the night with intense pain.

"I could hardly get out of bed and when I got out,
I could hardly walk," Sarah said. "I shuffled into the
chair with more moist heat and ice packs that I
alternated as the doctor told me to do, but I still hurt."

The pain was so severe that Sarah decided to read
her Bible, hoping to find comfort in its pages. Not
knowing what to read for her situation, she selected

some Psalms. But she was in such intense pain that she could hardly remember what the Psalms said.

After reading a few verses, Sarah prayed, not for healing, but simply for some relief from the intensity of the pain. *If only I could enjoy a few moments of peace at night,* she thought. After praying night after night for two weeks, Sarah noticed the pain slowly leaving her back. She also realized that she enjoyed her evenings as she never had before her injury.

Sarah took pleasure in the stillness of the house in the middle of the night, something she rarely got to enjoy in her busy day. She also enjoyed the little things she could now do without any pain, like rolling over in bed, walking on her own to the bathroom, or slipping out of bed for a drink of water.

The Psalms include many verses on healing. If you have physical pain, accept the strength and power that God will send to you in the night. Meditate on His Word and be prepared for the comfort He offers.

Green Pastures

*He makes me lie down in green pastures; he leads
me beside still waters; he restores my soul . . .*
Psalm 23:2-3 NRSV

One night Mary Lu's eight-month-old baby cried
every few minutes. Exhausted from the daytime chores
of motherhood, she didn't want to slip out of her
warm bed again, but she knew she had to make her
baby comfortable for the night.

She plopped her feet on the cold floor and dashed
to the nursery. In the dim night light, the first thing
Mary Lu noticed was that Brad's diaper, gown, and
tee-shirt were soaked. She took off his clothes, washed
him with warm water, dried his soft body with a fluffy
towel and sprinkled baby powder on him.

As she tended to Brad's needs, he kept fussing.
When Mary Lu tried to put a dry diaper on him, he
kicked it off. Finally she managed to fasten the diaper

before he could kick it off again and slipped a clean nightgown on him. Still the baby fussed.

"Shh," Mary Lu shushed, gently encouraging her baby to stop crying. *If only Brad could understand that in just a few minutes he'll be able to go back to sleep!* she thought in exasperation.

Finally, as Mary Lu rubbed his back and sang softly to him, Brad drifted off to sleep. Soon he was snoring softly.

On her way back to bed, Mary Lu suddenly thought of a Bible verse she'd never understood as a child: *He makes me lie down in green pastures* . . . (Psalm 23:2 NRSV).

She realized that although Brad didn't understand it, God used her to provide "green pasture" for him. She thought of the times when she fussed at God in the same way that Brad did at her, until later, when she realized God was actually blessing her and making her to lie down in green pastures.

Remember to rest and treat yourself to green pastures tomorrow. Take a walk in the park, read a good book, or visit a close friend.

A Cheerful Heart

A cheerful heart is good medicine, but
a crushed spirit dries up the bones.
Proverbs 17:22

Janelle became so distraught with the stress of deadlines in her work as an artist that she didn't know what to do. She decided to call her friend, Gail.

"Hello," Gail answered. At the sound of her voice, Janelle burst into tears.

"What's wrong?" Gail asked.

"Could you come over? I'm so depressed," Janelle said.

"Of course."

Within a few minutes, Gail sat on the edge of Janelle's bed. Janelle noticed that Gail held a book in her hands.

"What's that?" Janelle asked.

"A joke book."

"I'm not in the mood for jokes," Janelle.

"Let me just read you one," Gail suggested.

Janelle wasn't excited about the idea, but she agreed to listen to one joke. Gail read the joke. Janelle couldn't help but laugh.

Smiling, Gail's dark blonde eyebrows raised as she asked, "Can I read another one?"

Janelle shrugged. "I guess it can't hurt anything. You might as well go ahead."

So Gail read another joke. Janelle laughed again.

This continued until Gail had read about a dozen jokes. The laughter brought Janelle out of her depression. After Gail left, Janelle returned to her paintings with a renewed vigor.

Laughter is a gift from God to help us through the hard times in life. When we laugh, our bodies release endorphins, a substance that produces calmness in much the same way as a tranquilizer. That's why so many doctors say laughter is a great healing tool for the troubled soul. What a blessing we can be to others by sharing the gift of laughter!

Safe in His Arms

*And will not God bring about justice for his chosen ones, who
cry out to him day and night? Will he keep putting them off?
I tell you, he will see that they get justice, and quickly.*

Luke 18:7-8

One night just days before Christmas, a fire broke
out in the home of a family as they slept. One of the
girls, Carolyn, who was eight years old at the time,
woke up to a popping sound. She knew it wasn't a
sound that she was accustomed to hearing at night. So
she slipped out of bed to find the source of the strange
noise. As she dashed down the hall, she saw swirls of
smoke. Carolyn raced to the bedrooms of her parents
and siblings.

"Fire!" she screamed. "There's a fire in our house!
We've got to get out!"

Immediately, her parents and sister woke up,
jumped from their beds and ran out of the house. But
her brother, four-year-old Jason, remained fast asleep.
Outside, his parents noticed that their only son was
missing. They were panic-stricken.

Fearing the boy was still inside, his father headed for the porch as flames whirled up to ten feet in front of him. Before he opened the door, Carolyn burst out the front door, firmly holding Jason's hand. Braving dense smoke, she had gone back inside to find her little brother.

When the news media asked the girl why she had gone back into the burning house for her brother, she simply smiled and said, "Because I love him."

"She saved our entire family," her father said.

The mother smiled in agreement. The fire, which was started by a burning candle near the Christmas tree, destroyed the family's house.

"We're all safe, and that's what counts," the father said.

This typical family experienced the goodness of God in the middle of a disaster. He will do the same for you. And He just doesn't offer protection during the day; His protection extends into the night as well.

This evening, we can be thankful that God watches over us tonight. Relax knowing that you're safe in God's arms.

Comfort at Night

I stay awake through the night to think about your promises.
Psalm 119:148 TLB

Stressed to the max nearly every evening after a busy day caring for her two preschoolers, Samantha would crawl into bed at night, feeling as if she hadn't accomplished anything. Before marriage, she had worked as an accountant in one of the firm's downtown. Now she was a harried mother.

In contrast, her husband's career was flourishing. She was happy about his success, but at the same time she felt unimportant in comparison to him. While she spent the day chasing toddlers, her husband consulted with corporate presidents and designed skyscrapers.

"I envy you," Samantha said one night.

Kent's dark eyebrows shot up in surprise. "Why on earth would you be jealous of me?"

"Because you're so successful. Every day I do the same boring things. I don't do anything that's important."

"But you do so much!"

"Like what? Change dirty diapers?" Samantha felt even sorrier for herself.

Kent pointed out to his wife that every day she spent quality time with their children by reading them Bible stories, taking them swimming or to the library, making play dough, cooking three nutritious meals, and bathing them. On top of that, Kent continued, she also volunteered her time in the church nursery.

"Don't you think those things count?" he asked.

Samantha admitted that she had never thought about her life in that way. Instead of focusing on the joys of the present, she had mourned for the life she had left behind. That night, instead of going to sleep right away, she reflected on what her husband had said. She could always resume her career when the kids went off to school. God seemed to say, *Enjoy your family now while you can. Your children won't be little forever.*

Tonight you can do the same. Think of all the contributions you are making to others. And then sleep in peace, knowing that God is pleased with you.

Kindness Bouquet

A kind man benefits himself, but
a cruel man brings trouble on himself.
Proverbs 11:17

Not surprisingly, Kristina, a middle-aged woman who regularly practices kindness in her life, has a lot of friends.

One day Peg confessed to Kristina that she was depressed. Peg had two small children who required lots of care, and she worked part-time as a secretary to help with finances. She felt overwhelmed.

"The hardest thing I do is to get out of bed every morning," Peg said. "I'm so down that I don't know what to do."

Kristina immediately tried to think of some act of kindness to cheer up Peg. The first thing Kristina thought of was that her friend loved flowers. So out of her own backyard, she picked an assortment of wild purple, yellow, and red flowers that gave off a wonderful aroma and arranged them with a handful of wild greenery in a pretty vase.

When Kristina delivered the flowers to Peg, her friend's brown eyes lit up and she exclaimed, "Are those for me?"

"I decided you needed some flowers so that you'll know somebody cares about you."

Several days later, Kristina spotted Peg at the grocery store. "How are you feeling?" Kristina asked.

"Terrific!" Peg said with a wide grin. "You made me feel so special when you picked those flowers just for me." What Peg said next deeply moved and touched Kristina. "You know, I never appreciated the beautiful dandelion bouquets my children gave me," Peg said. "Now I look at them and see that in my busy world, there are so many tiny, beautiful things that I've never noticed before. It's a miracle really. I'm not feeling depressed anymore."

A little act of kindness can touch someone's life forever. Preparing dinner for a tired mother, running an errand for someone, or writing an encouraging letter to a friend are a few acts of kindness that we can incorporate into our lives. Not only can we make another person feel special, but we can feel pretty good about ourselves, too.

The Best Business Partner

Instead, you ought to say, "If it is the Lord's will,
we will live and do this or that." As it is, you
boast and brag. All such boasting is evil.
James 4:15-16

Can't sleep because you're worried about your business and financial situation?

That was the case for Bill, a middle-aged businessman who was always telling others that he would do this or that with his public relations business; it was always something that was sure to make money for him. Yet day after day, month after month, year after year, things never happened the way he predicted, and he felt like a failure. Finally, his business went bankrupt.

"At the time, I was devastated, thinking I'd never get back on my feet again financially," Bill said. "I felt desperate."

He did, however, regain financial independence. As a matter of fact, Bill became extremely successful in the business world. He credits his newfound success to having God as his business partner.

"I love people," he said. "But before, I was trying to make ends meet by figuring it all out with math, which I never liked that well in school. No wonder I struggled with my job."

Looking back, Bill says going bankrupt was the best thing that ever happened to him. It made him change his attitude. He began trusting God.

"Before, I was afraid to take risks . . . to try new things," he explained. "Now, if one way doesn't work in my business, I no longer look at that as failure. I see it as an opportunity to try something else."

If we're having a hard time making ends meet, we can review our situation and think of ways to change like Bill did. We can find work that we love. By doing our best at our jobs, being the best we can be, we can enjoy the life God designed especially for us.

Out of the Spotlight

For his anger is but for a moment; his favor is for
a lifetime. Weeping may linger for the night,
but joy comes with the morning.
Psalm 30:5 NRSV

As a teenager, LuAnne entered a national
beauty pageant. She'd won several other beauty
contests; she was blessed with beautiful, long-brown
hair, dark-brown eyes, a trim figure, a sense of humor,
and a natural intelligence. This was the first time,
however, that she would compete nationally.

More than anything, LuAnne wanted to win the
pageant. She figured taking home a national title
would boost her self-esteem and that it would
eliminate all her problems . . . at least most of them.

The night of the contest, LuAnne carefully applied
her make-up and slipped into a long, flowing, pink
chiffon, evening gown. On stage, she smiled widely
and walked with elegance. For the talent portion, she
sang better than ever.

Later, the announcer read, "And the winner is LuAnne . . . . " The applause roared in her ears. She was so thrilled. *Finally,* she thought, *I'm somebody!*

But when LuAnne returned home, she soon realized that she still had problems just like everyone else. In fact, her life was filled with more stress than before the contest. She traveled around the country, giving speeches while trying to maintain high academic grades. In addition, she had to meet deadlines for television and newspaper interviews.

After months and months of a hectic schedule, LuAnne felt drained of all energy. She looked forward to the day when her reign as a beauty queen would end and a new girl would take her place. She wanted her old life back so that she could spend time with her friends.

Soon the year passed, and a new queen was selected for the upcoming year. LuAnne was more than happy to step out of the spotlight.

Our stress-filled problems may seem to offer no solutions, but there is hope. We *can* find joy and peace. We may have to struggle first through the night, but joy comes in the morning. That's one of God's promises. What a beautiful one!

Nighttime Warmth

When the dew settled on the camp at night,
the manna also came down.
Numbers 11:9

One evening a babysitter struggled to persuade three children, ages four, three, and one, to go to sleep. Holly tended to the one-year-old first. She fed him a bottle as the two older children raced back and forth in the living room. It had been several hours since their parents had left, and she was exhausted.

"Sh!" she said to the older children. "If you'll be quiet so I can get your baby brother to sleep, I'll read you a bedtime story."

The children's mother had told her that the older children, Melissa and Jim, loved bedtime stories. When Holly promised to read to them, Melissa and Jim immediately settled down at the mention of story time.

After feeding the baby, Holly rocked and sang softly to him as he drifted off to sleep. Carefully, she rose from the rocking chair and carried the baby into the nursery, laying him down in his crib.

To her surprise, she discovered Melissa and Jim had already settled in their beds with several books piled around them, ready for Holly to read.

"Will you read us a story now?" Melissa asked, wrinkling her freckled nose.

"You promised," Jim reminded Holly.

"Yes, I did." Holly chuckled at the children's enthusiasm. She settled in between the two children and opened the first book. While reading the third story, both children fell asleep.

Holly crept out of the room and curled up with a warm blanket on the sofa. She felt good, knowing that she had done her best for the children and they were safely tucked in their beds for the night. She sighed and thanked God for the way the night had gone. Listening to the comforting ticking of the grandfather clock, she enjoyed the stillness of the night and opened up her own book.

Tonight, curl up in a warm blanket, drink a cup of hot chocolate, and relax with a good book. Savor God's manna in the Bible.

Don't Stand So Tall, Daddy!

*How great is the love the Father has lavished
on us, that we should be called children of God!*
1 John 3:1

"Don't stand so tall, Daddy," the little freckled-face boy cried in the grocery store aisle. No matter how many times he pulled on his father's pants leg, he couldn't get any attention. Tears rolled down his face, as his father seemed to ignore his pleas.

"Don't stand so tall, Daddy!" he cried again, but much louder this time. The man finally leaned down in front of his son and looked at him eye to eye, listening intently. A smile lit up the little boy's face, replacing his tears.

The child reached out and held his father's face with his little hands. "I love you, Daddy," he said.

"I love you too, son," his father said simply.

The man stood up and resumed his shopping. Happy and content, the little boy followed in his father's footsteps. He had only needed the assurance of those special words—*I love you.* He wanted to know for sure that his father loved him.

How many times have we simply needed someone to offer a kind word or a gentle hug to get us through a trying situation? When insecurities arise or when our days abruptly turn to night, those three little words can mean so much. *I love you!* We all need our loved ones to come down to our level where we can confide in them.

Even though God is all-powerful and stands tall over our world, when we call upon His name, He reaches down and communicates with us heart to heart. He shows His love for us through His Word, in the beauty of the universe, and in the miracle of life. When we kneel in prayer, God's Spirit draws near to us to whisper those special words—*I love you.* We never grow too old to appreciate the assurance of His love.

A Special Mission

*And whoever welcomes a little child
like this in my name welcomes me.*
Matthew 18:5

Sam's wife hadn't attended a worship service for more than thirty years. Sunday after Sunday, the elderly deacon walked in and found his seat alone on the second pew. Newcomers thought he was single, but the established members knew the truth. He was a dedicated soul who lived his life serving and praising His Father in heaven. He passed out candy to the little ones and expressed his love freely among the members of the quaint church.

Although his wife, Helen, wasn't present during the worship service, she was there in spirit with her husband. She also supported the pastor with her prayers and fattened him up with her delightful chocolate desserts. Over the chatter of little mouths

and the screaming of infants, she faithfully listened to his sermons by intercom.

Sam and Helen were always the first ones to arrive for every service. Helen had an important job to do and took it quite seriously. As director of the church nursery, she wanted to be early and ready before the little ones arrived. Each and every day of the week, she lifted her babies up in prayer before she retired for the night. She loved each special one as if it were her own.

Many women offered to relieve her, but she wouldn't allow it. God had called her to this service, and it was her intention to continue with it as long as possible. Over the years, "her" babies grew to adulthood and presented her with children of their own. She was truly loved by all.

As she rocked and sang to each child, she was serving her God in a powerful way. She provided a safe and warm environment for the little ones, while their parents fed on the Word of God.

God has a job for each of us. This woman found hers in the care of tiny babies. Tonight, ask God how you can serve Him best.

His Grace Is Amazing

*My grace is sufficient for you, for
my power is made perfect in weakness.*
2 Corinthians 12:9

The room was silent except for the labored
breathing of the child and his mother's tender voice
singing the familiar words of *Amazing Grace*. Most of
the day had been difficult as the young boy's fever
soared. Panic invaded their home when he convulsed
in seizures due to his extremely elevated temperature.

Even though his condition seemed stable for now,
Karen continued to hold him close while rocking to
the tune of their special song. Leaving his side tonight
would be impossible. She felt that as long as she was
holding him close to her heart, he would be safe and
sound until morning. In the still of the night, his tiny
eyes briefly fluttered open. He didn't feel like

speaking. But when his eyes met his mother's, she saw hope, as a tiny smile appeared on his pale face.

"Thank you, Jesus," Karen whispered. The sound of her Lord's name created a sense of serenity in the room. A feeling of peace and calm assurance took residence in Karen's heart. She knew that God was near and that He was holding the two of them close to His side. She could rest, assured that He would never leave her alone. Just as her son could count on her undivided attention, she could count on God's everlasting presence. His Word is true even though sometimes life's problems seem too heavy to bear. She drifted off to sleep, as her faith sustained her.

God's amazing grace was sufficient through the night. As the sun finally peeked over the horizon, sunbeams filled the room with radiance. Karen knew that the worst was over when her little boy opened his eyes and caressed her face with his tiny hands. A new day, with a new reason to praise God, was born.

Jesus gives us His amazing grace, which is sufficient for today and forever.

Only the Best

Therefore God exalted him to the highest place
and gave him the name that is above every name.
Philippians 2:9

When God sprinkled the stars across the universe, He knew exactly where He wanted to place each and every one. He took control of the gravitation of earth, the tilt of its axis, and the orbit of the moon. Knowing exactly how much heat the world would need, He provided the sun and all of its glory.

God even thought of little things when He formed the universe. He knew that His children would enjoy snow sometimes and warm weather at other times. He knew that the joy of nature would bring peace and contentment to hearts and souls everywhere. God also thought of the fact that without a mate, His children could become lonely. He wanted only the best for His creation, so He planned out everything carefully.

He wanted to be sure that when the nights seemed too long and the days too short His children could continue to experience peace, so he provided many wonderful gifts along the way. The gift of salvation is the most wonderful present that could ever be offered or received. He provided the sacrifice in the form of a man—a perfect man, no less. His name was Jesus, the Name above all names. He lived, died, and lives again, and that enables us to live forever.

Because He lives, beauty can be found in the darkness, just as it can be found during the daylight hours. Looking at the stars and seeing the glow of the moon can bring joy to the soul of man. Sleepless nights can become blessings if God's children use that time to seek His face.

The power of God can be magnificent in the quietness of the night. His presence can be felt in an uplifting way through prayer and worship. He is worthy of our praise, even when the night seems long. It's through the difficulties that we learn to trust the sweetest name on earth—Jesus.

In His Time

In the time of my favor I heard you,
and in the day of salvation I helped you.
2 Corinthians 6:2

As a new Christian, Tricia wanted to know everything about God. She prayed that He would reveal Himself and His truths to her so that she could live her new life in a productive way. Even though God listened to her prayers, He didn't instantly answer her every request.

Instead He taught her the things she needed to know to get through each and every day. He held her hand as she lived her life as a wife and mother. Many times Tricia thought she saw His eyes when she looked into her children's eyes. During trials and difficulties, she felt His powerful but gentle touch. Unusual events occurred that convinced her of His everlasting presence.

Little did she realize that during those times, she was growing closer to God daily. When she listened to sermons and gospel music, her soul was being watered. She needed the living water in her life, just as much as her backyard garden needed the nutrients and hydration of physical water. During difficult times in her life, she needed extra fertilizer to aid her spiritual growth. That fertilizer came in the form of Bible study classes and the teaching she received in Sunday school.

As the years passed quickly, Tricia's babies left home and her parents' health began to fail. While her husband worked long hours, she began to discover her inner self. Writing became much more than just a hobby. It became her mission and her service for God. She spent hours tapping at the keys on her computer. Through her letters, columns, and stories she touched the hearts of many souls. Tricia never failed to give God the credit.

During those times when you feel as though God has not answered your prayers for the moment, remember that He works on a different time schedule than we do. Ask Him to show you how you are being changed . . . day by day.

God's Treasures

*Come to me, all you who are weary
and burdened, and I will give you rest.*
Matthew 11:28

$\mathcal{U}$p on the hillside in a quiet community stands
a quaint little country church. Its steeple stands
proud, and its stained-glass windows provide a
welcoming atmosphere to everyone who passes by. As
the wind blows, the tall trees bow down over the
church, as if they are protecting the outside walls of
the magnificent but small structure.

On Wednesday nights and Sunday mornings, the
church comes alive with enthusiasm and laughter, as its
dedicated members come to worship God. During that
time, love is evident as friends and family members
embrace each other with warm hugs and handshakes.

During the week, the church is normally quiet.
Periodically, someone will stop by to walk around the

yard, while admiring the beauty it bestows. This place is truly God's house, a holy and sanctified building. Many times a passerby will slow his pace and see the beauty it holds, but sadly too many people speed by without even acknowledging its existence.

Unfortunately, these people regard God in the same manner as they do His church building. Their days are too busy. They speed through life without seeking His Will for their life or enjoying His everlasting love for them. As God looks upon the earth, He probably sheds a tear knowing that some of His children are simply surviving life rather than living an abundant life. He offers a life full of hope and peace.

God will not force a person to stop to smell the roses, to ponder the history of His house, or to worship Him. But when a passerby glances toward the church and lifts a few words to Him, He rejoices with the angels in Heaven. Like salvation, the opportunity to stop, to rest in His hands, and enjoy the treasures that God gives is available to all who will take the time to accept His gift.

A Very Important Man

*Whatever you do, work at it with all your
heart, as working for the Lord, not for men.*
Colossians 3:23

The school custodian looked like a very
important man to the young boy. "Mr. Jones has more
keys than anyone I know," he told his teacher one
beautiful spring day. He was amazed at all the keys
that Mr. Jones carried on his belt.

"He is an important man," his teacher told him. "He
takes good care of our school and makes sure that
everything is in good working condition. He comes
early in the morning, while you're still asleep, to make
sure that we have a safe and clean building in which to
learn. His nights are short, and his days are long."

At about that time, the bell rang, and the children
raced out to recess in the school yard. Immediately,
Mr. Jones stepped into the quiet classroom.

"Hi," the busy custodian said. "I'll only be here a few minutes. I want to take out your trash and pick up a few things while the kids are outside."

"Thank you for all you do," the teacher said. "You do a great job."

"Give the praise to God," Mr. Jones replied, as he continued with his work.

Miss Robinson watched as he hurriedly swept and dusted, trying to finish before the children returned. As he worked, he hummed old-time gospel tunes. Once finished, he didn't hesitate before going to the next room. The teacher stepped outside her door and watched as he made his way down the hall, cleaning everything in sight with enthusiasm.

After recess, when all of the children were back at their desks, Mr. Jones walked past their room down the hallway. The teacher heard the clanging of the keys and realized that although many keys hung from his belt, the greatest key that he carried was the key to the kingdom of God. His example revealed to all what really makes a man important: the love he has for God and his devotion to others is surely the key to happiness and success.

Jailhouse Rock

*Believe in the Lord Jesus, and you will
be saved—you and your household.*
Acts 16:31

The jailer was exhausted. It had been a busy day, and the graveyard shift just didn't seem to suit him that particular night. After receiving orders from higher authorities to make sure that Paul and Silas didn't escape, the jailer did everything humanly possible to keep them in a secure place.

Paul and Silas were not in a comfortable environment. They realized, however, that they were going to be there for a while and that they might as well make the best use of their time. Somehow, it seemed like the ideal time to sing hymns and pray to God.

With all the enthusiasm they could muster, Paul and Silas rocked the jailhouse with praises to the King of kings. Many of the other prisoners listened intently.

With all the singing and praising going on, they couldn't sleep anyway. The jailer finally fell asleep, despite the enthusiastic singing of Paul and Silas. When an earthquake shook the building and the doors flew open, the jailer was ready to give up. At the point of losing it all, the jailer gained the most important truth that he could ever have discovered. The gift of salvation was offered and gladly accepted on that sleepless night by him and his entire family.

Have you felt like giving up lately? Have your nights been filled with storms and problems in recent weeks? Have you accepted the wonderful gift of salvation? Maybe it's time to allow the Rock of Ages to enter your heart. Just as God was with Paul and Silas that night in the inner dungeon, He wants to be with you through all of your difficulties.

Chains bound the two followers of Christ. What kind of chains are binding you? God has the solution to all of your problems and the key to set you free. Sing His praises and watch carefully as He leads you out of life's dungeons and into His everlasting arms of love.

Light in the Storm

*I am the light of the world. Whoever follows me will
never walk in darkness, but will have the light of life.*
John 8:12

The day was full of light! The waves tumbled
against the shore in a most inviting way, while a slight
breeze made the palm trees shudder with delight.

The scuba diving club decided it was a great day
for an underwater adventure. Everyone geared up
excitedly. After the leader assigned buddies, the group
descended into the crashing waves. The newest
member, Jim, was particularly eager because this was
his first real dive. He had practiced in small bodies of
water many times, but seeing the ocean floor was a
dream come true.

After offering a brief goodbye to his family, he
walked out into the ocean. Then seemingly out of
nowhere, a storm blew in. Pellet-like raindrops fell as

thunder crashed. Lightning popped all around. Everyone scattered, seeking shelter. About an hour into the storm, Jim's family panicked. The other divers were returning, but Jim had not been seen anywhere.

His family and friends began to pray. After another half-hour, he came running toward the car through the darkness of the storm. It turned out that when he had returned to the surface of the ocean, the storm was so heavy and the clouds were so dark that he couldn't see the shoreline. So he dropped his gear and swam toward a glowing light, which guided him to safety.

That day Jim learned some important lessons about life and scuba diving. Sometimes when storms break out, a person must be willing to let go of the weights that hold him down. No matter how valuable the scuba gear, Jim's life was more important. He never replaced the equipment, but allowed it to rest forever on the ocean floor.

His love for his family and God increased greatly as a result of the dive. He realized, too, that during even the bleakest hours of life, God's light is the light that leads to life.

The Power of Prayer

*And the prayer offered in faith will make the
sick person well; the Lord will raise him up.*
James 5:15

As the day turned into night, Renee welcomed
the time for rest. Taking her small son to the hospital
to endure a battery of tests had made her day difficult.
Exhaustion had set in, and her nerves were frayed.
While the doctor felt that the test results would be
good, she was still concerned. After putting the baby
into his crib, tears flowed down her face when she left
his room.

The ringing of the telephone startled her. Before
she answered it, she tried to control her tears but
found that it was impossible. When Renee answered
the phone, the caller—a wise woman named Carol—
realized immediately that Renee was upset. Carol
asked if she could pray with her. After she agreed,

Carol prayed the sweetest prayer Renee had ever heard. Carol then told her that she loved her and assured her that things would be all right.

As Renee placed the receiver back on the hook, she had a new outlook regarding her son's health. Somehow she knew that God had heard every word that had been spoken during that prayer, as Carol had interceded with Him to bless Renee's family. She had the assurance that all would be well.

As the sun rose the next morning, Renee awoke with a new sense of peace. Confidently, she dialed the doctor and received wonderful news. All the tests were negative. Her son would be fine.

"Thank God!" she shouted, grateful that He had heard her prayer.

Prayer is the most powerful force in the world. It serves as a direct line to God. It also serves as a time to celebrate happiness and success, giving God the full credit for all of our accomplishments. Prayer is a privilege and a wonderful gift given by a loving God. Day or night, He's always available to listen to every word.

The Promise of the Cross

*For the message of the cross is foolishness to those who are
perishing, but to us who are being saved it is the power of God.*
I Corinthians 1:18

"You might need to come," the nurse said. After
receiving calls such as this on many occasions during
the last six months, Lorraine was exhausted. Her days
were difficult, and her nights were long as she worried
about her father. Six months earlier he was diagnosed
with a terminal illness.

The seventy miles to the nursing home was a long
trip, especially during desperate times such as this
one. On her previous trips, her father was stable by
the time she arrived. This time, however, the nurse's
voice sounded different. Her heart was heavy, and her
eyes were tired.

While driving, she shouted questions at God. She
couldn't understand why God would allow this to

happen. She tried to serve Him faithfully, but she felt that God had deserted her and her father.

"Why don't You love me anymore, God?" she cried. Just as the words left her mouth, a bird flew up from the cotton field beside the interstate. It fluttered in front of her windshield and then flew straight up. Her eyes followed as it flew toward what appeared to be a cross in the sky.

Instantly she realized that God had just answered her plea. *I do love you,* He seemed to say. *I sent my Son to die for you. Remember the cross!* She began to weep, as she asked for forgiveness for her wavering faith. When she arrived, the nurse met her at the door with good news. Her father's health had once again stabilized.

That event happened almost two years ago, and although her father's health is deteriorating gradually, her faith in God has never faltered again. God told her that He loved her, and that's all she needed to hear.

When her father goes home to be with the Lord, Lorraine is convinced that God will be at her side to hold her up and keep her strong. The promise of the cross is eternal.

Things That Go Bump

I will lie down and sleep in peace, for you alone,
O LORD, make me dwell in safety.
Psalm 4:8

"I'm going to be brave tonight," the eight-year-old told herself as she was getting ready for bed. "I am going to sleep in the dark whether I'm afraid or not." For several months she had tried to accept the darkness without fear, but night after night "the things that go bump" got louder and louder.

As Emily crawled under the covers, her eyes were as big as saucers. Darkness filled every corner of her room. She was determined not to be afraid, until all at once she heard that bump. She jumped up, wondering what was in her room that had caused all the commotion.

"I knew it was going to happen!" she cried out.

Emily jumped up and switched on her night-light, revealing her familiar toys and dolls. She returned to bed with a lighter heart and a sense of peace and fell asleep right away. There's something comforting about the light that chases away fear from a child's mind.

Being in physical darkness is not pleasant. But one thing that's worse is living an entire lifetime in spiritual darkness without the love and companionship of Jesus Christ. Without Him, the sun doesn't shine bright enough, and the stars aren't as special as they twinkle in the heavens above us. Without Him, the world is a lonely and desolate place, filled with things that go bump in the night.

When Christ enters the heart of man, a transformation takes place immediately. The shadows lift, and a new joy replaces the fear that once possessed the soul. The night doesn't frighten us anymore. Knowing He's in control provides peace and contentment.

A Dream Come True

As you know, we consider blessed those who have persevered. You have heard of Job's perseverance and have seen what the Lord finally brought about. The Lord is full of compassion and mercy.

James 5:11

Peck, peck, peck, the typewriter sounded late into the night. Mary Beth was so tired that she turned over and put her pillow over her head, trying to muffle the sound. *I've told him about waiting until the last minute,* she reasoned. *I'm not getting up this time. He can do it himself.*

Peck, peck. The typing continued.

Jack wanted to be a teacher, but because they married, he never got around to taking the courses he needed to make his dream a reality. After several years of marriage and all the children had started school, Mary Beth went back to work so Jack could return to college.

Between the two of them, they worked six jobs, with Jack also attending school full-time. This was his last quarter, his last term paper, his last assignment.

Well, if I can't sleep, I might as well type, she fumed, getting up to face the day early.

The paper was due at eight o'clock that morning. With forty-five minutes and only one paragraph to go, the typewriter ribbon ran out.

Frustrated, Mary Beth jumped into the shower. When she walked back through the room, her husband was busy printing the last paragraph on the paper. She was sure the professor would take points off for it. She left for her job, still tired and frustrated. Later that day, he called her at work.

"I couldn't have done it without you, honey," he said. "I got an A."

"Congratulations," she said, wondering why the teacher didn't deduct any points.

Later he explained that his teacher had compassion on him. The teacher knew they had worked hard through the night and that sometimes problems just happen. Mary Beth's forgiveness enabled him not only to receive a diploma but also to realize his dream of becoming a teacher.

Do you need God's compassion tonight? He's always waiting to help His children.

Abiding Love

*In your anger do not sin: Do not let the
sun go down while you are still angry.*
Ephesians 4:26

The constant pain in Valerie's hips made her
days and nights almost unbearable. She tried to
control her temper, but it flared at the most
inappropriate moments. Nobody escaped—not the
cat, not the kids, not even her husband. Night after
night, she would wake up her longsuffering husband,
asking him to help her turn over.

One day after trying to mop the kitchen floor, she
turned to Peter. "Could you help me?" Calmly, he
took the mop from her and finished mopping. Later
as she stood at the kitchen sink, she fumbled with the
dishes and pain shot through her hips. She had just
finished the silverware when her husband took a dish
from her hand.

"Go sit down," he said. "I'll finish these."

Valerie's face flushed, and she felt frustration burning her cheeks. She really hadn't wanted to trouble him with her problems, yet she was relieved to get off her feet.

"You know, honey, I can't read your mind," he said. "If you want me to help, all you have to do is ask." Peter winked at her and put a saucer in the dishwasher.

After taking her medication, Valerie felt some relief before going to bed. Free from much of the pain, she focused on Jesus and His compassion for those who had afflictions. Soon, she realized she had shown no compassion to the man who married and cherished her.

In a moment, the Lord revealed that Peter had shown her the highest love of all—unconditional love—the kind that God expresses. When her husband crawled into bed that night, she leaned over and kissed his cheek. "Can you forgive me?" she asked.

He smiled and said, "I've already forgiven you."

How amazing to know that God knew and loved us while we were still in the womb. He knows who we are and why we act as we do in our humanness, yet through His grace, He loves us anyway.

A Child of God

How great is the love the Father has lavished on us, that we should be called children of God! And that is what we are!
1 John 3:1

Pamela brushed her hair from her eyes and looked at the red numbers on her digital clock. It read 3:00 a.m. She heard her daughter, Tina, call again.

"Mama, I'm sick," said the child, coughing.

The young mother tugged on her bathrobe and hurried to her daughter's bedroom. Feeling her daughter's forehead, she realized the fever had risen again. With sleep still stalking her, Pamela got a thermometer and a cool cloth. "Let's take your temperature, honey," she said.

With the fever up to one hundred and three degrees, she gave Tina some medication to bring the fever down. Once again, the child began to cough—a barking, croupy cough. After five minutes of nonstop coughing, her little girl couldn't seem to catch her breath.

A Child of God

Frantically, Pamela picked up her daughter and raced into the bathroom. She turned on the hot water, letting it steam the room. For a few minutes, the child continued the coughing until the warm, moist air relaxed her constricted throat. Tina snuggled close to her mother. As a ritual before sleep, the little girl twisted a piece of sandy-colored hair, as her eyelids drooped.

Pamela carefully lifted her daughter, walked to the bedroom, and laid her down in bed. "Mama," begged her daughter, "please don't leave me."

She wished she could go back to her own bed, but Pamela's maternal instinct was stronger than her own need for sleep. She slipped beneath the covers alongside her daughter. Gently, she gave Tina a loving and reassuring hug. As the child began to doze, Pamela realized that this must be how God cares for us.

Knowing how much God cares for us brings an inexplicable peace. When we call to our Father, He hears, and in His infinite wisdom, He answers. He comes alongside of us and embraces us in our greatest hour of need. How much our heavenly Father loves us!

Christmas Revelation

Thanks be to God for his indescribable gift!
2 Corinthians 9:15

It was Christmas Eve, and rain pattered on the rooftop. The mother of two teenagers had lain awake until her sons were home, and now she couldn't sleep. She curled up in her recliner, facing the decorated tree.

Memories of other Christmases flooded back like the rain that cascaded down the window. It wasn't long ago that she'd been divorced and alone with her little boys. That sad year, every apartment except theirs was decorated for Christmas.

A friend had given her a small tree, which she and the boys had decorated without much enthusiasm. Being new in the community, in addition to being divorced, she hadn't had the time, nor the inclination, to visit a nearby church. So she was alone . . . and lonely.

As Christmas neared, the pine tree's needles grew brittle and brown. On Christmas Eve, her seven-year-old son said, "Mom, the needles are falling off!"

Everywhere she stepped, she felt the prick of a pine needle. The boys giggled every time she had to sit down and rub her feet. Finally, she and her sons lugged the tree to the curb.

On Christmas morning, they sat cross-legged in front of the coffee table and shared their inexpensive gifts, while in the background the radio played "Away in a Manger." She looked at her two small boys and said, "I wish I had more to give you."

"It's all right," one of her son's said. "At least we have each other."

As the memory faded, she looked toward the nativity scene, focusing her thoughts on baby Jesus. "And now," she whispered, as a smile lifted the corners of her mouth, "we have the gift of Jesus in our lives."

What a blessing God gave us—the indescribable gift of His Son, Jesus Christ—the gift of a Savior . . . a present of flesh and blood.[22]

Sharing God's Comfort

Praise be to the God and Father of our Lord Jesus Christ, the Father of compassion and the God of all comfort, who comforts us in all our troubles, so that we can comfort those in any trouble with the comfort we ourselves have received from God.

2 Corinthians 1:3

Cathy shares God's comfort with everyone she meets, especially those who have experienced the ravages of cancer. She knows much about the disease. Not only had she undergone surgery for breast cancer in 1990, but she also had experienced its return—with a vengeance—a year later. At that point, the only option the doctors gave her was to have a bone marrow transplant.

After much prayer, Cathy decided in favor of the transplant, which forced her to stay in isolation for six weeks in an Atlanta hospital. She was bombarded with massive doses of chemotherapy twenty-four hours a day for four days and given blood transfusions. She was so weak from the assault on her body that she could barely speak.

Her friends in Christ responded to her need by offering prayer, encouraging cards, poetry, phone calls, and food for her family. As a result, Cathy returned home as an encourager and became an important part of her cancer support group at the local hospital, where she spent countless hours helping others.

Once, not long after her bone marrow transplant, Cathy offered support to a single mother with recurrent breast cancer. The mother faced a procedure called stem-cell recovery. Knowing the mother had no other help, Cathy drove her to the hospital in Atlanta and sat with her through numerous long and painful tests. During one of the tests, as Cathy waited patiently by her bed, the woman embraced her and said, "Thank you so much for all you've done."

Since then Cathy has uplifted and encouraged numerous people facing similar cancer treatments. Cathy has been cancer-free for several years now, and she continues to comfort others as God comforted her in her hour of need.

Cathy acknowledges that God's Spirit used her friends that year to help lift her spirit. Now He works through her life to bless others. Tonight, ask God if there's someone with whom you can share His comfort. Pass it around!

Who's in Control?

Peace I leave with you; my peace I give you.
I do not give to you as the world gives. Do not let
your hearts be troubled and do not be afraid.
John 14:27

*W*endy jumped at the opportunity—two full weeks alone to write. Looking forward to her "writer's retreat," she eagerly packed her car with everything she would need and drove away from her house. Finally she reached her destination—a cabin on a deserted road, almost hidden by overgrown bushes.

That first evening, Wendy watched the sun dip behind the hardwood forest, leaving in its wake blackness so dense that, without moonlight, she couldn't see her hand in front of her face. Inside the cabin she refused to think about being alone in the middle of the woods and calmly stacked her writing books, dictionary, and paper next to the computer she had brought along.

Later, she worked on a poem, then stretched out on the loveseat. Picking up a novel, she began to read. Yawning sleepily, the words on the page blurred, and she dozed off. Some time later, a noise in the attic awakened her. She bolted upright, her heart pounding in her ears. *Lord,* she thought, *please take this fear from me.*

Her breathing quickened as she walked silently to the bottom of the stairs and looked up at the locked attic. Easing up each narrow step, she felt a lump in her throat. Listening at the attic door, she realized to her great relief that the sound was merely mice scurrying across the wooden floor.

The next morning, Wendy thanked God for His ever-present help in time of trouble. Holding a mug of coffee, she walked down a pathway to the woods. Sun-dappled wildflowers greeted her, and lizards raced under rhododendron bushes. Around the next turn was a hidden waterfall. She sat down on a boulder and prayed, turning all her fears over to God, trusting Him to take care of her. During the rest of her stay at the cabin, her writing flowed as easily as the rush of water over river rocks.

Tonight, if you need peace, seek God's.

Have You Forgiven?

But if you do not forgive men their sins,
your Father will not forgive your sins.
Matthew 6:15

One day Corrie ten Boom visited a friend in the hospital. Though her friend was quite ill, Corrie noticed that she also was quite bitter.

At first, the two women spent time catching up on each other's lives. Finally the woman said that her husband disliked having a sick wife, and as a result, he had left and was living with a younger woman. Knowing that her friend was greatly distressed, Corrie asked, "Have you forgiven him?"

The woman said, "Certainly not!"

At first Corrie had trouble believing that her friend had not forgiven her husband. Then she remembered a time when she herself had been unforgiving. After World War II, she had recognized a nurse who had been cruel to her dying sister while they were detained in the Ravensbruck concentration camp. The memories flooded back, and she recalled how her sister had suffered because of this nurse.

In that moment, Corrie knew that she had not forgiven. She knew she must forgive, but she couldn't seem to bring herself to do it. She finally had a talk with God.

"Lord," she said, "You know I cannot forgive her. My sister suffered too much because of her cruelties." The Lord revealed Romans 5:5 to Corrie: *The love of God is shed abroad in our hearts by the Holy Spirit which is given unto us* (KJV). Then she prayed, "Thank You, Father, that Your love in me is stronger than my bitterness."

When she finally met the nurse, Corrie told her that although she had been bitter about what happened to her sister, that now Corrie loved her. By the end of their conversation, Corrie shared the way to salvation, and the nurse accepted Jesus Christ as her Lord and Savior.[23]

Forgiving someone else is powerful. It is a blessing to the one forgiven, but it also releases the one forgiving from the bondage of bitterness. If you need to forgive someone tonight, ask God to show you how.

Disaster Relief

Whatever you do, work at it with all your heart,
as working for the Lord, not for men, since you know
that you will receive an inheritance from the Lord
as a reward. It is the Lord Christ you are serving.
Colossians 3:23-24

Rose-Marie Oostman, a 53-year-old grandmother, looked in dismay at the Gainesville, Georgia, landscape that early morning in 1998. Her first impression of the deadly tornado's devastation was one of disbelief. The two-hundred-mile-per-hour tornado had raked a path through the area that measured ten miles long and a quarter mile wide.

"I saw hills strewn with debris as far as you could see," she said. "Houses were gone. You had to be there to fully appreciate the immensity of it."

Part of the cleanup and recovery team, she and other Georgia Baptist disaster relief volunteers cleared away more than ten trees that covered one family's trailer. They worked for days, ministering to the immediate needs of the victims.

Having experienced a fire years before that destroyed everything she owned, Oostman didn't hesitate to help others. When she learned of the disaster relief ministry, she wanted to be involved and received training in the use of chain saws.

Oostman met a man that day who had served in Vietnam. He awoke at four o'clock the morning of the tornado and sensed a need to pray for his family. When the tornado hit, his home and family were spared. After realizing they were safe, he and his wife began helping others.

According to Oostman, one survivor said, "I didn't think we'd have any help. I thought we'd be here all by ourselves." But Oostman knew that as long as her group stayed together as a team, they would be there. She and the other volunteers poured out God's love to the community that day, thus living up to the ministry's motto—"Serving Christ in the Crisis."

When we help those who are in immediate need, we can show God's unconditional love to an unbelieving world. We might not receive many service awards for helping others. But God will know and reward us in Heaven.[24]

Following the Shepherd

My sheep listen to my voice; I know them, and they follow me.
John 10:27

Phillip Keller, author of *A Shepherd Looks at Psalm 23*, was raised in East Africa where he fell in love with the life of a shepherd. As a young man, he was a sheep owner who loved wildlife and spent countless days caring for his sheep.

Intimately acquainted with sheep and their habits, Keller wrote about cast-down sheep. A cast-down sheep is usually one that is heavy or long-fleeced. The sheep searches an area until it finds a spot where it can lie down comfortably in a depression in the ground. When it rolls onto its side, the sheep finds its body shifting. Soon the sheep is trapped on its back, unable to get up.

When the cast-down sheep is a ewe with lambs, it can be a great loss to the owner if she is not found in time because the unborn lambs will die with her unless the shepherd is there to help.

Many times, Keller counted his sheep and learned one was missing. His first thought was, *One of my sheep is cast down somewhere. I must go in search and set it on its feet again.*

One day Keller found a cast-down ewe. He gently rolled her over on her side, lifted her to her feet, and straddled the sheep with his legs. Gently, he rubbed and restored the circulation in her limbs. As he worked, he would speak gently, "When are you going to learn to stand on your own feet?"[25]

Many of us look for soft, comfy spots in which to live. We like to believe that we have it made. But therein lies the greatest danger. Often, we find ourselves cast down like sheep, unable to get to our feet by ourselves. Tonight, let the Good Shepherd, Jesus Christ, who knows and hears your voice, lovingly lift you to your feet.

The Gift of Forgiveness

For the wages of sin is death, but the gift of
God is eternal life in Christ Jesus our Lord.
Romans 6:23

It was two weeks before Christmas when Nikki drove toward the mall to exchange Christmas gifts with her friend. A sense of dread hung over her, much like the dark clouds that were threatening rain. A light drizzle began falling, and she switched on the windshield wipers.

For more than eight years she and Barbara had shared the Christmas holiday at a favorite restaurant, but this year a disagreement had brought on hurt feelings. On the car radio she listened to the songs of the season, but nothing could cheer her up.

Pulling into the parking space, she turned off the engine, wishing she'd never agreed to this lunch. Inside the restaurant, Nikki walked toward a small table near a window. Soon, she saw Barbara drive up, and she steeled herself for a difficult lunch.

"Sorry I'm late," said Barbara, placing a gaily-wrapped package on the table.

Both women ordered salads and continued with small talk until they finished their meal. Finally the time came to share their Christmas gifts. Nikki handed Barbara a gift bag while she studied the carefully wrapped package she was given. Almost in tandem, they opened their gifts. The gifts paled in comparison to what transpired next as the friends were parting.

Nikki picked up her gift, relieved that the awkward occasion was over. Just then, Barbara reached out to her in love, and they exchanged a long, heartfelt embrace. "Thanks so much for the present," Barbara said. "We need to do this again really soon."

As Nikki drove home, she noticed the clouds had lifted and the sun was trying to peek through. She smiled, realizing what she and Barbara had really exchanged was the gift of forgiveness.

Has your heart been mired in hurt, anger, or disappointment? Allow God to give you a new spirit for forgiving those who have hurt you.

God's Provision

If you remain in me and my words remain in you, ask whatever you wish, and it will be given you. This is to my Father's glory, that you bear much fruit, showing yourselves to be my disciples.

John 15:7-8

Ed Butchart's ministry began in 1981 when he made friends with a man who had cerebral palsy. To his surprise, Butchart found himself helping to change a lightbulb, which was something the man couldn't do himself. It gave Butchart a feeling he'd never experienced—a feeling of sacrificially helping others. From this small beginning, his nonprofit wheelchair ministry started.

Butchart's ministry has grown from a small space in his garage to a 64,500-square-foot warehouse that houses wheelchairs, wheelchair parts, and other similar devices.

In the beginning, Butchart and his wife, Annie, worked tirelessly rebuilding the wheelchairs themselves. Now the ministry boasts a paid staff of eleven, many of whom live with disabilities. Kevin Riggs, the ministry's director of communications and a quadriplegic with cerebral palsy, is responsible for designing the ministry's Web site and writing brochures.

Miracles are a way of life at the ministry. Once a mother and her physically challenged son asked for a 386 personal computer. Before Butchart could explain they didn't have one, a truck unloaded a number of computers. Among them was a working 386 model, which Butchart gave to the family.

A few days later, the mother and son came back. "I can't believe this place," the mother said. "You make dreams come true. . . . " When the woman hesitated, Butchart asked, "What's your other dream?" The woman asked for a van equipped with a wheelchair lift. But she didn't want just any van, she wanted a Volkswagen van.

Butchart smiled. "Will blue be OK?" In the back of the building stood a blue Volkswagen van, which he repaired before giving it to them.

God has opened countless doors for the ministry, especially during many times when the coffers were empty. After Butchart and his staff pray for finances, God provides what is needed, usually within days. A modest man, Butchart takes no credit but gives all the credit to God.[26]

Tonight, ask God how you can help others.

Food in My House

Bring the whole tithe into the storehouse,
that there may be food in my house.
Malachi 3:10

"What? You just lost your job?" Deborah took a deep breath, then sat down quickly. She watched the laugh lines at the corners of her husband's eyes turn somber. Although her husband had been a faithful employee of the same company for more than twenty-six years, he was let go when the company's earnings dropped. Deborah watched as her husband mentally battled the onslaught of depression.

"Hey," she said. "I'll take you out to eat tonight."

"Why?" he asked. "I just lost my job."

"Because I'm trying to keep you from getting depressed," she said. A grin spread across his face, and she knew she had hit pay dirt.

Later at the restaurant as they sat across the table from each other, her husband leaned forward and whispered, "I think I'm going to be very depressed next Friday."

The woman felt her throat clutch. "Oh," she said.

"Yeah, I think we'll have to go to another restaurant so I'll feel better," he joked.

When they got home, the first thing they did was pray together, asking specifically for God's guidance. Her husband began sending out resumes and making phone calls.

Months dragged on, and depression crept into their lives after they received little response from prospective employers. But when Deborah heard about Hurricane Mitch's devastation in Honduras, she immediately gathered clothes and canned goods for the victims. Her husband stopped her. "What are you doing? That's our food."

"Those people need clothes and food more than we do," she said. "I also think we should give ten percent of your unused vacation pay to them." After writing the check, the Lord released a flood of joy in both of them. The next day, two companies called to schedule an interview. A month later, one of them offered him a job.

Sometimes we have trouble letting go of our material wealth to help others. Yet God promises that He will abundantly provide all that we need.

Unfailing Love

The LORD delights in those who fear him,
who put their hope in his unfailing love.
Psalm 147:11

Writer Marion Bond West wrote about "The Healing Tree" when things weren't going right and she doubted her roles as wife and mother. At the time, her self-reliant older daughter was pregnant, she and her teenage daughter couldn't seem to get along, and the twin boys preferred their father.

One afternoon, she asked her husband if he wanted to go for a walk. "No," he said in a matter-of-fact way.

Disappointed, West drove to the woods and walked by herself. The only sounds were her own footsteps and rushing water in a stream. In the distance, she saw a lone black walnut tree. At its base, she sat down. The wind churned and leaves detached from a branch. *How easily this tree lets those leaves go,* she said to herself. *If only I could let go as easily.*

Thinking of her husband, West picked up a branch. She prayed to release those things about him that troubled her and tossed the stick into the water. Picking up a smaller stick, she thought, *Please let me stop controlling my daughter's life.* She threw the stick as far as she could.

One by one, she released her children to the Lord. A larger stick represented her pregnant daughter. *Don't let me be meddlesome in her affairs, Lord.* She dropped the stick into the water.

Then she picked up twin sticks. *Don't let me press the boys into what I think they should be,* she prayed, tossing both sticks into the swirling water.

The last stick was hers. *Lord,* she prayed, . . . *there's so much in me that is selfish and demanding . . . love my family with Your unconditional love.* She dropped her stick into the stream. Immediately, she felt a sense of freedom from her bondage of worry.

There's freedom in releasing our loved ones to the Lord. When we stop clinging to past anger and disappointment, we experience the Lord's unfailing love and acceptance.[27]

Hearing God's Voice

Be still, and know that I am God; I will be exalted among the nations, I will be exalted in the earth.
Psalm 46:10

The last time Allison saw her sister Beth, they had a difference of opinion and decided to go their separate ways. She later learned her sister had turned her back on God.

As the years passed, Allison missed her younger sister and unsuccessfully tried to find her. For a long time, she pleaded with God to help her find Beth. Finally, she stopped begging God to answer her prayers and placed the request in His hands to do what pleased Him. The days, months, and years passed, and it seemed as though her prayers would remain unanswered.

But God had heard her prayers. Two weeks before Christmas in 1998, Allison busied herself decorating the house in the stillness of the late afternoon. As she placed the nativity on top of the television set, her thoughts turned to the first Christmas and the Christ-child who was God's love gift to the world. How she wished she could share that love with her sister.

Glancing out the window, she saw the mailman stuff another batch of cards into the mailbox. Wrapping her sweater around her, she went outside. All of the envelopes, except one red one, had return addresses. Curious, she turned it over and opened it.

"Please forgive me, Sis," it read. "I apologize for not getting in touch sooner. I hope we can talk." Allison looked at the enclosed photos, and tears sprang to her eyes. Fifteen years was a long time.

When the sisters finally spoke to each other, Allison was surprised to learn that her once-wayward sister was now a Christian. "I still have the Bible you gave me when I was six," Beth said. "It's still in the original box, and not only that, I use it." To Allison's surprise, God had shared His love gift of Jesus with her sister.

Tonight, put your trust in God and let Him take care of your family.

Nothing Is Impossible

I tell you the truth, if you have faith as small as a mustard seed,
you can say to this mountain, "Move from here to there"
and it will move. Nothing will be impossible for you.
Matthew 17:20

When Jama Hedgecoth was five, she found a hungry cat. Even at that age, Jama loved animals and couldn't stand to see any animal in need. She begged her mother to let her keep it. When her mother said no, Jama placed her balled-up fists on her hips and said, "Mama, one of these days the Lord is going to give me all the animals I want."

The daughter of traveling evangelists, Jama believed strongly in God. Years later, her faith became reality. Today, Jama is married, with four children, and lives on one hundred and twenty-two acres of farm country in Georgia, where she began Noah's Ark, a safe haven and rehabilitation center for more than a thousand animals.

When Jama first saw the property, she knew without a doubt that God would give it to her. Her husband's response was one of disbelief when Jama started packing. As boxes piled up, her husband called her father and said, "Jama has lost it. She's packing, saying God's going to move us to the property. We don't have a penny. I can't even find my socks. . . . "

Jama's father merely said, "If God spoke to her, just hang on." And God did give the property to them.

Jama's faith remained strong. Once when Noah's Ark was near financial ruin, an Atlanta businessman offered to pay off the center's mortgage and build a foster children's home, where twelve children are housed.

Through her faith in God, Jama has taken in animals that nobody else wanted, including wildcats, lions, monkeys, and emus. And she has opened up her heart to foster children. She even plans to build two more homes: one for the elderly and one for terminally ill children.

Sometimes God wants us to step out in our faith—not to prove to Him that we have faith but to prove to ourselves how much we believe in the power of our God.[28]

In Jesus' Name

*My purpose is that they may be encouraged in heart
and united in love, so that they may have the full riches of
complete understanding, in order that they may know
the mystery of God, namely, Christ, in whom are
hidden all the treasures of wisdom and knowledge.*

Colossians 2:3

Thirty-seven-year-old Joyce Girgenti, a Christian artist, shares her faith by painting the name of Jesus into her inspirational paintings.

One year, Joyce was approached by an organization who wanted her to donate a Christmas card scene. Her first effort, a fireplace scene complete with a Christmas tree and nativity, was turned down. Undaunted, Joyce replaced the scene with another, and it was accepted. Later, Joyce realized why her original scene was rejected; God had other plans.

Joyce had used a photo of her own fireplace to paint the original scene. Working from the top of the canvas, she painted the Christmas tree, the nativity on the mantel, the roaring fire, and the stones that formed the fireplace. As she began to paint the bottom of the fireplace, she turned to her daughter. "Wouldn't it be neat to hide something in the fireplace that refers to Christmas?" she asked.

Before her daughter could answer, Joyce said, "What better than Jesus? He's why we celebrate Christmas." She then arranged the fireplace stones to spell out the name of Jesus. At her daughter's urging, she added a stone that resembled a heart.

After her card was rejected, Joyce used it to send to clients and friends. One day, Joyce received a call from her friend, Mary, who asked, "Is Jesus' name really in your fireplace?" She had called to verify what she'd found.

In each of her inspirational paintings, Joyce seeks to please God by painting Jesus' name somewhere in her work. She shares her faith with everyone she meets, saying, "If you forget me, you've lost nothing, but if you forget Jesus, you've lost everything."

It's a mystery trying to find His name so well hidden in Joyce's paintings, but the real mystery is not His name—it's Jesus Himself. Only when Jesus is revealed are we able to discern His hidden treasure for us—His gift of salvation.

A Flash Prayer

Dear friends, since God so loved us, we also ought to love one another. No one has ever seen God; but if we love one another, God lives in us and his love is made complete in us.

1 John 4:11-12

Nan stood at the window one winter day watching the wind whipping the pine trees. The cold rain had sneaked in the night before. Early that morning, she had struggled to get out of bed as the extreme cold and dampness wreaked havoc on her joints.

At the post office, everyone seemed to feel as she did. No one smiled, and everyone seemed to be struggling through their day. She decided then and there to at least change her own outlook. She smiled—not a forced smile, but a caring smile that radiated the love of God. For some, she whispered a "flash prayer" that their day would be blessed by the heavenly Father.

Her smiles brought blessings from God in the form of a grandmother who rushed to her side to share a funny story, a man who asked her opinion on which handbag to buy for his wife, and the boy who allowed her to take his place in the express lane.

Nan remembered how a smile began a friendship with a young, grocery-store bagger with Down's syndrome. One winter day, with snow clouds slung low across the sky, the young man carried her groceries to her car. Digging in her purse for a tip, she was embarrassed when she found she had nothing to give him.

"I'm sorry," she said, not wanting to disappoint the young man.

A smile as bright as the summer sun spread across his face. "That's okay," he said. Then he wrapped his arms around her. "I love you," he said. Shivering in the cold, she whispered a "flash prayer" for this special child of God. "Lord, bless this precious child," she whispered.

Sometimes the most unexpected encounters can teach us a lesson in humility, but the greatest lesson in humility is found in Jesus Christ.[29] Tonight, whisper a "flash prayer" for someone you saw today.

The Secret Gift

*But when you give to the needy, do not let your
left hand know what your right hand is doing, so
that your giving may be in secret. Then your Father,
who sees what is done in secret, will reward you.*

Matthew 6:3-4

It was the Christmas that Diane's son, Marty,
was eight that she witnessed a miracle. Her youngest
child, Marty was filled with an unquenchable spirit
even though he had a minor handicap. He was deaf in
one ear.

While times had been difficult for her family,
Diane knew how much better off she was than Kenny's
mom, who lived nearby and struggled daily just to
feed and clothe her children.

Several weeks before Christmas, Diane realized that
Marty was saving his small allowance for a gift to give
Kenny. One day he strolled into the kitchen and
showed her a pocket compass. "I've bought Kenny a
present," he said.

Knowing how proud Kenny's mother was, Diane didn't believe she would allow her son to accept a gift if he couldn't give one in return. Marty argued with his mother and finally said, "But what if it was a secret? What if they never found out who gave it?"

Diane finally relented and watched her son walk out the door on Christmas Eve, cross the wet pasture and slip beneath the electric fence.

He raced up to the door and pressed the doorbell, then ran down the steps and across the yard so he wouldn't be seen. Suddenly, the electric fence loomed in front of him, and it smacked him hard. The shock knocked him to the ground, and he gasped for breath. Slowly, he got up and stumbled home.

Diane treated the blister on Marty's face, then put him to bed. The next day, Kenny came to the front door excitedly talking about his new compass. Amazingly, Marty seemed to hear—with both ears.

Later the doctor confirmed that Marty somehow had regained hearing in his deaf ear. Though the doctor said it might have been the shock from the electric fence, Diane believed that miracles still happen on the night we celebrate our Lord's birth.[30]

A Mountain Man's Faith

*Then I heard the voice of the Lord saying, "Whom shall I send?
And who will go for us?" And I said, "Here am I. Send me!"*
Isaiah 6:8

Henry "Harrison" Mayes, born in Fork Ridge, Tennessee, in 1898, was almost crushed to death in a coal-mining accident. Following the accident, Mayes, a mountain man, spent a lifetime serving God.

When the mine caved in, he was crushed so badly that the doctors didn't think he'd live through the night. The physicians called his family in while he was semi-conscious. Harrison Mayes rallied long enough to say, "I promise the Lord if I get through this, I will spend the rest of my life serving Him."

Against all odds, Harrison Mayes did survive. His first thought was to start preaching, but his wife said he did a terrible job of it. "By the time he got through preaching," she said, "there wasn't half a dozen people left in the church. He knowed right away that wasn't what he was called to do."

A Mountain Man's Faith

Mayes found that his real talent lay in painting signs. He was a man dedicated to serving God, and one of his first signs was painted on a pig in large black letters—SIN NOT. He sent the pig into the coal-mining camps where miners sat drinking moonshine.

Later Mayes began lettering wooden signs with "Jesus Is Coming Soon" and "Prepare to Meet God" and placed them along the highways. Before long, he made wooden molds to create fourteen-hundred-pound concrete crosses and heart-shaped signs. Before his death in 1986, he had placed these eight-foot-tall crosses and hearts along highways in every state in the country except four.

With only a fifth-grade education, Mayes was so dedicated to serving God that he constructed a lighted cross 140 feet tall and 60 feet wide that stands overlooking Middlesboro, Kentucky. Even today, it proclaims a mountain man's message of faith.

The Lord still asks, "Whom shall I send?" Tonight, what is your answer? Will you say, *I'll think about it later,* or will you be like Isaiah? His response was, "Here am I. Send me!"[31]

Stormy Weather

*For God did not give us a spirit of timidity, but
a spirit of power, of love and of self-discipline.*
2 Timothy 1:7

Elizabeth stared out the window at the low-hanging rain clouds. Kissing the top of her newborn's head, she snugly wrapped the blanket around him, wishing her husband were home. The child opened his slate-blue eyes and cooed. As her heart filled with love for this new human being, she felt an inexplicable warmth pass between them. She wondered if perhaps this was the way God felt about His children.

By nighttime the rain had turned into a tap-tapping sound, and Elizabeth realized it was now sleeting outside.

"I'll bet you want something to eat," she said, touching the baby's cheek. She placed him on his side in the playpen and gave him a warmed bottled, then began to pace the floor.

Later, the sleet turned to freezing rain. Peeking outside, she could see the ice-coated pine trees bowing to their knees. Nervously, she said out loud, "Jim, where are you?"

Just as she started toward the telephone, the lights went out. She lit the Christmas candle on the mantel. The house quickly chilled. She wrapped another blanket around the baby and put a cap on his head, then pulled on her coat.

What if the lights don't come back on soon? What if they don't come on for days? Her mind raced through all the possibilities. Where was her husband? In all this bad weather, had he been in an accident? "Oh, Lord," she whispered, "I'm so afraid."

In the darkness and deepening silence, she heard an inner voice remind her that God is our refuge and strength, an ever-present help in trouble. Within the hour her husband came home, and not long after the lights blinked on.

God says in His Word, the Bible, that we should not give in to our fears, but we often do. This night, cast your doubts and fears at the foot of the cross, and let the outstretched arms of Jesus Christ wrap you in His peace.

Active Trust

Do not let your hearts be troubled, Trust in God; trust also in me.
John 14:1

In her book *Beyond Our Selves,* Catherine Marshall writes about her husband, Peter Marshall, and his active trust in God. A popular Presbyterian minister, her husband served as chaplain of the U.S. Senate during the late 1940s.

Catherine once said, "I thought that faith was believing this or that specific thing in my mind. Now I know that faith is nothing more or less than actively trusting God." To demonstrate this, she provided an illustration her husband used:

"Suppose a child has a broken toy. He brings the toy to his father, saying that he himself has tried to fix it and has failed. He asks his father to do it for him. The father gladly agrees, takes the toy and begins to

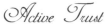
work. Now obviously the father can do his work most quickly and easily if the child makes no attempt to interfere, simply sits quietly watching, or even goes about other business, with never a doubt that the toy is being successfully mended.

"But what do most of God's children do in such a situation? Often we stand by offering a lot of meaningless advice and some rather silly criticism. We even get impatient and try to help, and so get our hands in the Father's way, generally hindering the work.

"Finally, in our desperation, we may even grab the toy out of the Father's hands entirely, saying rather bitterly that we hadn't really thought He could fix it anyway . . . that we'd given Him a chance and He had failed us."[32]

Are you placing your loved ones in the generous hands of our Father, who knows what is best for His children? Or are you clinging to them, believing only you can protect them? Try putting your trust in a Father who tends His flock like a shepherd, gathering His children in His arms and carrying them close to His heart.

Sweet Dreams

Unless the LORD builds the house, they labor in vain who build it; unless the LORD guards the city, the watchman stays awake in vain. It is vain for you to rise up early, to sit up late, to eat the bread of sorrows; for so He gives His beloved sleep.
Psalm 127:1-2 NKJV

As a nurse, Linda had worked the day shift for years. When her supervisor changed her schedule to the night shift Linda thought, *No problem.*

It wasn't long, however, before Linda discovered she had a hard time getting to sleep during the day. Then, after several hours or more of trying to fall asleep, when she finally drifted off, her telephone or doorbell often would ring and wake her.

Linda would return to bed only to toss and turn throughout the day, trying to find a comfortable sleeping position. So when evening arrived and it was time for her to go to work, Linda would be exhausted.

She knew she had to do something so she could get enough sleep. She hooked up an answering machine to the phone and placed a "Please do not disturb" sign on the door. Even so, the ringing phone still woke her and aggressive door-to-door salesmen ignored the door sign. No matter what she tried, nothing seemed to work.

Then one day she read Psalm 127. "I read the scripture, and I knew the *He* in the verse was God and *His beloved* was me," Linda said. "So I started saying that verse when I got in bed during the day to go to sleep. And soon I'd be sound asleep."

As the days passed, the same thing happened over and over. Linda would recite the verse, think about it for awhile, and drift into sleep. Today, she has no problem sleeping during the day as she manages her evening work shift and personal family life.

When you go to bed tonight or tomorrow morning, think about that verse. God has promised that He will give you, His beloved, the rest you need. Claim His promise!

Nightlight

The Lord went in front of them in a pillar of cloud by day, to lead them along the way, and in a pillar of fire by night, to give them light, so that they might travel by day and by night.

Exodus 13:21 NRSV

Six-year-old Mark was afraid of the dark. He didn't like being in his room at night without a light on, but he was afraid to tell anyone about his fear because he thought they would laugh at him. So every night Mark would get into bed and lie awake for an hour or more before he could fall asleep.

As weeks passed, Mark's fear of the dark increased. He'd go to bed only to have his heart pound as he tried to get to sleep. Even though he was embarrassed about his fear, Mark decided to tell his mother. He didn't know what else to do. So one night when bedtime came, he said, "Mom, I hate going to bed."

"Why?" his mother asked.

Mark spoke in a soft voice, "I'm afraid of the dark."

Then, to Mark's surprise and delight, his mother didn't laugh. She lovingly put her arms around him and said, "How about if we find some light for you at night?"

"How would we do that?" he wanted to know.

After she hugged her son, Mark's mother said, "I can put a bedtime light in your room."

"I don't know if that will help," Mark said honestly.

"Isn't it worth a try?"

"Yeah," Mark shrugged, "I guess."

So Mark's mother went to the store and bought a night light. That evening she turned it on. A warm golden glow lit up Mark's room. He grinned and said in an excited voice, "Look Mom! I can see a bunch of stuff with that small light! I'm not afraid now!"

As the next few evenings passed, Mark had no problems with the dark because of the ray of light that spread across the room from the small nightlight.

The light of God's guidance doesn't end at sundown. We can take assurance that God will keep right on looking after our needs, directing us—giving us light—even through the night.

Fifty-six Friends

*Two are better than one, because they have
a good reward for their labor. For if they fall,
one will lift up his companion. But woe to him who is
alone when he falls, for he has no one to help him up.*

Ecclesiastes 4:9-10 NKJV

One evening a drug addict admitted during an Alcoholics Anonymous meeting that he often felt the need to have a drink in the middle of the night. Mark had to find a way to keep from drinking, because he knew his alcoholism was a matter of life and death. He sought the help of his fellow alcoholics.

"I'm going to pass my phone book around the room," Mark told the others in the room. "If any of you wouldn't mind getting a call from me in the middle of the night, please jot down your name and phone number."

Mark emphasized to the attendees that if they had any misgivings, he didn't want them putting their phone numbers in his book.

"I want to be able to call you without feeling guilty," he explained, "and, of course, if you don't want to be disturbed during the night, I understand that, too. You don't have to sign the book."

As the book circulated throughout the room, Mark saw people digging into their pockets and purses for pencils. The room was silent while he waited for the phone book to be returned to him. Mark couldn't help but wonder how many people would sign the book.

Moments later, the last man to sign the book handed it to Mark. When Mark opened the book, he began to cry. He discovered he had some really good friends—lots of them.

Fifty-six people were at the meeting. Fifty-six people signed his book.

On his way home, Mark rejoiced, knowing he could receive help at night by calling one of his new friends, people that God had brought into his life. That kind of friend is a treasure—a blessing to our lives. A friend is one we can call in the midst of our despair, no matter what time of night. And we can be treasures in return, by offering a listening ear in the middle of the night.

Bringing the Sunshine Back

The LORD gives strength to his people;
the LORD blesses his people with peace.
Psalm 29:11

It was one of those wet rainy days at the end of winter, in that interlude between the cold weather and the warmth of spring, a time of daffodils peeking their bright yellow blossoms through the ground and offering promise of more to come.

In a small house on the corner, Rhonda, a young mother of three, was fixing lunch for her children. Their favorite sandwich was peanut butter and jelly. She brought the bread and peanut butter out of the cabinet and removed the blackberry jelly from the refrigerator. The lid on the jar of peanut butter seemed to be stuck tight. She tried and tried to open it, but the lid wouldn't budge.

Suddenly, Rhonda burst into tears. She had reached her limit. The baby had cried all night with colic, so she had gotten little rest; the two-year-old was his usual "terrible twos" self; the rain meant the kids couldn't play outside, and now the dumb lid to the peanut butter jar wouldn't come off.

At about that time, her five-year-old daughter came into the kitchen. Kylie had been playing with dolls in her bedroom when she heard her mother crying. The little girl hugged her mother around her waist and said, "Don't cry, Mommy. God will bring the sunshine back tomorrow."

Kylie's words put everything back into perspective for Rhonda. She knew that she had overreacted because she was so tired. Kylie was right. Tomorrow was another day.

Most of us can probably put ourselves in this young mother's place. We've all felt we were at the end of our rope at some time or other. Sometimes the smallest incident causes us to spill over, making us believe we can't cope anymore. Whatever the situation, always remember that God—in the words of a small child—will bring the sunshine back tomorrow.

Starry, Starry Night

*The heavens declare the glory of God; and
the firmament sheweth his handywork.*
Psalm 19:1 KJV

Remember when you were a child, lying on your back outdoors, staring up at the celestial stream of stars and moon? All was peaceful and still. How relaxing it was to quietly gaze at the shimmering lights and simply dream! Even as an adult, you are not too old for that. Everyone needs a quiet time to be alone with God, without television, radio, or teaching tapes. If you can't find quiet time, it's because you've given it away. But you can take it back now.

God created you more special than all other things, even the stars in heaven. The psalmist wrote in Psalm 8:3-5, *When I consider thy heavens, the work of thy fingers, the moon and the stars, which thou hast ordained; What is man, that thou art mindful of him? And*

the son of man, that thou visitest him? For thou hast made him a little lower than the angels, and hast crowned him with glory and honour (KJV).

God has a special place in His heart just for you and wants you to know Him in a more intimate way. The Lord desires this relationship even more than you do. Having your friendship pleases Him.

Don't listen to the lies of the enemy, who tells you that God is angry because you haven't read your Bible lately. As you spend time with God, you will be strengthened. This strength will keep you from throwing in the towel when times get tough. Make your quiet time top priority. Consider it an appointment with God. Mark on your calendar now the time you plan to spend with God each day and give it first place.

Cloaked in Darkness

*He made darkness his secret place; his pavilion round
about him were dark waters and thick clouds of the skies.*
Psalm 18:11 KJV

*O*ur darkest hour is often the prelude to a great
victory. God invades our circumstances and hides us
with His cloak.

Late in the night on Monday, August 24, 1992,
America's most destructive hurricane, Andrew,
slammed into the east coast of Florida near Miami.
Fierce winds measuring up to one-hundred-and-sixty-
four miles an hour blasted a path of destruction across
the peninsula. Andrew's fury left behind broken glass,
buckled doors, split ceilings, roofs ripped from walls,
and soaked furniture blown blocks away.

Many who stayed to face the worst of the raging
winds hid in small windowless bathrooms, with entire
families shielded by mattresses, hoping the storm
would spare them. Those who evacuated returned
only to wonder where they were. "It was horrible,"

Jeanette said, reliving the pain. "I couldn't find my house in all the wreckage. Nothing was recognizable. It looked like a nuclear weapon hit."

A veil of darkness and fear fell upon Jeanette and her family. Facing the shock of Andrew's damage, they realized the awesome power of this natural disaster. After experiencing the trauma of the storm itself, they found their day-to-day life was becoming more and more difficult. It was in the midst of this fury that God moved in. "Left with only the clothes on our backs, we knew God had saved us. We refused to be beaten, and God gave us the strength and courage to not give up," Jeanette said.

In this seemingly hopeless situation for Jeanette's family, God flooded their lives by meeting all of their needs. "The Lord provided for us in miraculous ways, and every day became brighter," Jeanette recalled.

Many are faced with situations like Jeanette's, such as the devastation left behind by natural disasters like floods, tornadoes, and hurricanes. If you are one of those, ask the Lord to flood the darkness with His light. As the raging storms swirl around you, God will burst forth with the light of His presence.

The Power of Forgiveness

Be angry but do not sin; do not let
the sun go down on your anger.
Ephesians 4:26 NRSV

When an elderly woman's only son was
murdered, she told her minister that she would not let
anger creep into her life over the tragedy. Even so,
Susan realized that she had done the very thing she
vowed not to do. Hatred filled her heart.

For some time, she was unable to sleep at all. One
night God spoke to her, not in an audible voice but in
a thought that she knew came directly from the
Father. He told her that if she wanted to start sleeping
well again, she needed to get rid of her anger and
forgive her son's murderer.

Susan was so disturbed that she slipped out of bed
and sat in a chair to pray. "Lord, how can You expect me
to forgive the man who killed my only son?" she asked.

She will never forget what happened next. God spoke to her again through a thought. He said, "I had to forgive a lot of people for killing My only Son."

As the tears streamed down her face, Susan asked God to forgive her for the anger and hatred she had carried in her heart. A powerful peace came over her. She went back to bed and fell asleep.

And, indeed, it did. Susan visited her son's murderer in prison and told him that she forgave him for what he had done to her son. The man's jaw dropped, and tears flooded his eyes. The two eventually became good friends.

People have asked Susan how she could have forgiven the man who took her son's life. She emphasizes that it was God who gave her the power to forgive. Today Susan is a happy woman who sleeps well at night.

If you find yourself unable to sleep tonight, review the contents of your heart. If it harbors any anger, ask God's forgiveness. Then go back to bed . . . and sleep well.

❀

No Need For Night?

*There will be no more night. They will not need the
light of a lamp or the light of the sun, for the Lord God
will give them light. And they will reign for ever and ever.*

Revelation 22:5

What is Heaven like?

No doubt most people, if not all, have wondered
about that at some point in their lives. Many of us
even turned to the book of Revelation in the Bible to
find out.

Even so, no matter how hard we try, we can't
totally comprehend living in a place where night
doesn't exist. It's difficult to visualize an environment
where there's enough light for everything all the time.
In Heaven, we will have no need for electric lights,
lamps, flashlights, candles or even the light of the sun,
moon, and stars!

A nightless place where light floods our
surroundings at all times is an awesome concept. Yet,
this is exactly how Heaven is described in the Bible.

No Need For Night?

Probably most people agree that from what the Bible says, Heaven sounds like a great place to live. Besides no night, the Bible says there won't be any tears, pain, or suffering in Heaven. Instead, all of us will experience joy, peace, and comfort besides beautiful mansions, gold streets, and sparkling jewels.

At times, we may think that such a place sounds too good to be true. We may wonder, *What's the catch?*

The good news is, there is no catch. God has promised we will have the opportunity to spend eternity in a state of happiness in Heaven . . . if we will believe in His Son, Jesus.

Tonight, reflect on Heaven and the happiness we're bound to receive when we get there. Think about seeing your friends and relatives in Heaven without having to struggle through any painful arguments and quarrels that lead to hurt feelings. We simply won't have any grudges to hold. We will live in harmony with everyone. There will be no need for soldiers having to go to war because everyone will be at total peace with each other.

What could be a more beautiful thought for us this evening?

References

Unless otherwise indicated, all Scripture quotations are taken from the *Holy Bible, New International Version* ® NIV ®. Copyright © 1973, 1978, 1984 by International Bible Society. Used by permission of Zondervan Publishing House. All rights reserved.

Scripture quotations marked NKJV are taken form *The New King James Version* of the Bible. Copyright © 1979, 1980, 1982, by Thomas Nelson, Inc.

Scripture quotations marked KJV are taken from the *King James Version* of the Bible.

Verses marked TLD are taken from *The Living Bible,* copyright © 1971. Used by permission of Tyndale House Publishers, Inc., Wheaton, Illinois 60189. All rights reserved.

Scripture quotations marked RSV are taken from *The Revised Standard Version Bible,* copyright © 1952 by the Division of Christian Education of the Churches of Christ in the United States of America and is used by permission.

Scripture quotations marked NRSV are from the *New Revised Standard Version* of the Bible, copyright © 1989 by The Division of Christian Education of the National Council of the Churches of Christ in the USA. Used by permission. All rights reserved.

Scripture quotations marked AMP are taken from *The Amplified Bible. Old Testament* copyright © 1965, 1987 by Zondervan Corporation, Grand Rapids, Michigan. *New Testament* copyright © 1958, 1987 by The Lockman Foundation, La Habra, California. Used by permission.

Endnotes

1. *Tales of the Shimmering Sky,* Susan Milord (Charlotte, VT: Williamson Publishing, 1996), p. 47.

2. *The Best-Loved Poems of the American People,* selected by Hazel Felleman (New York: Doubleday, 1936), p. 305.

3. *Black Heroes of the American Revolution,* Burke Davis. (New York: Harcourt Brace Jovanovich, 1976), p. 23.

4. *It Is Well with My Soul,* Horatio Gates Spafford, 1873.

5. *Artists Who Created Great Works,* Cathie Cush. (Austin, TX: [Raintree Steck-Vaughn Company, 1995), pp. 24-25.

6. *Carlsbad Caverns Silent Chambers, Timeless Beauty,* John Barnett. (Carlsbad, NM: Carlsbad Caverns-Guadalupe Mountains Association, 1981), p. 2.

7. *More Hot Illustrations for Youth Talks,* Wayne Rice. (Grand Rapids, MI: Zondervan, 1995).

8. *A Young Patriot: The American Revolution as Experienced by One Boy,* Jim Murphy (New York: Clarion Books, 1996), p. 47.

9. Adapted from *The Upper Room,* January-February, 1999. January 30, 1999.

10. Jason Cheng. Adapted from *The Upper Room,* January-February, 1999. January 22, 1999.

11. Mirlinda Boja. Adapted from *After Hours Inspirational Stories,* December 1998.

12. Donald C. Everhart, *The Upper Room,* January-February 1999. January 10, 1999.

13. Nathaniel Hawthorne. From *After Hours Inspirational Stories,* December 1998.

14. Adapted from *Daily Wisdom,* January 26, 1999.

15. Wayne Rice. Adapted *Daily Wisdom,* January 25, 1999. Edited from *Youth Talks,* Youth Specialties, 1994.

16. Kelly McHugh. Adapted from *The Upper Room,* January-February, 1999. January 9, 1999.

17. Patricia D. Brown. *365 Affirmations for Hopeful Living,* August 17.

18. George Prins. Adapted from *Daily Wisdom,* January 29, 1999.

19. Author unknown. Adapted from *Story Page for Teachers, www.geocities.com,* March 12, 1998. Quotation by William H. Danforth.

20. *Sequoia & Kings Canyon: The Story Behind the Scenery,* William C. Tweed. (Las Vegas, NV: KC Publications, 1980), pp. 2-29.

21. Kathleen Lowthert. Adapted from *The Upper Room,* January 29, 1999.

22. *After the Storm,* Nanette Thorsen-Snipes. (Wilson, NC: Star Books, 1990), pp. 22-23.

23. *He Cares, He Comforts,* Corrie ten Boom. (Old Tappan, NJ: Fleming H. Revell, 1977), pp. 29-33.

24. Nanette Thorsen-Snipes, *Georgia Magazine,* June 1998, pp.12-17.

25. *A Shepherd Looks at Psalm 23,* Phillip Keller. (Grand Rapids, MI: Zondervan, 1974, pp. 59-69

26. Nanette Thorsen-Snipes, *Christian Reader,* to be published December 1999.

27. *Look Out Fear, Here Comes Faith!,* Marion Bond West. (Ann Arbor, MI: Servant Publications, 1991), pp. 155-158.

28. Nanette Thorsen-Snipes, *Georgia Magazine,* 1999 (to be published).

29. Nanette Thorsen-Snipes, *Southern Lifestyles,* Summer 1996, p. 38.

30. Diane Rayner, *The Best Stories from Guideposts.* (Wheaton, IL: Tyndale House Publishers, 1987), pp. 219-222.

31. Nanette Thorsen-Snipes, *The Cumberland Trading Post,* November 1991.

32. *Beyond Our Selves,* Catherine Marshall. (New York: McGraw-Hill, 1961), pp. 87-88.

If you have enjoyed this book, or if it has
impacted your life, we would like to hear from you.
Please contact us at:

Honor Books
Department E
P.O. Box 55388
Tulsa, Oklahoma 74155
Or by e-mail at info@honorbooks.com

Additional copies of this book and other titles
in the Quiet Moments with God series and the
God's Little Devotional Book series
are available from your local bookstore.

Breakfast with God
Coffee Break with God
Daybreak with God
Sunset with God
Tea Time with God

God's Little Devotional Book
God's Little Devotional Book for Couples
God's Little Devotional Book for Dads
God's Little Devotional Book for Graduates
God's Little Devotional Book for Men
God's Little Devotional Book for Moms
God's Little Devotional Book for Students
God's Little Devotional Book for Teens
God's Little Devotional Book for Women

Honor Books
Tulsa, Oklahoma